The Atlantic Ocean

MANAGING EDITORS
Amy Bauman
Barbara J. Behm

CONTENT EDITORS
Amanda Barrickman
James I. Clark
Patricia Lantier
Charles P. Milne, Jr.
Katherine C. Noonan
Christine Snyder
Gary Turbak
William M. Vogt
Denise A. Wenger
Harold L. Willis
John Wolf

ASSISTANT EDITORS
Ann Angel
Michelle Dambeck
Barbara Murray
Renee Prink
Andrea J. Schneider

INDEXER
James I. Clark

ART/PRODUCTION
Suzanne Beck, Art Director
Andrew Rupniewski, Production Manager
Eileen Rickey, Typesetter

Library of Congress Number: 88-18337

2 3 4 5 6 7 8 9 0   97 96 95 94 93 92

Library of Congress Cataloging-in-Publication Data

Sharp, Peter J., 1944-
  [Oceano atlantico. English]
  The Atlantic Ocean / Peter J. Sharp

  — (World nature encyclopedia)
  Translation from the Italian of: Ocean atlantico.
  Includes index.
  Summary: Describes the plant and animal life of the
Atlantic Ocean and its interaction with its environment.
  1. Marine ecology—Atlantic Ocean—Juvenile literature.
2. Marine biology—Atlantic Ocean—Juvenile literature.
[1. Marine biology—Atlantic Ocean. 2. Marine ecology—
Atlantic Ocean. 3. Ecology—Atlantic Ocean. 4. Atlantic
Ocean.] I. Title. II. Series: Natura nel mondo. English.
QH92.S4813 1988 574.5′2636′09163—dc19   88-18338
ISBN 0-8172-3325-3

Cover Photo: Abarno

WORLD NATURE ENCYCLOPEDIA

The Atlantic Ocean

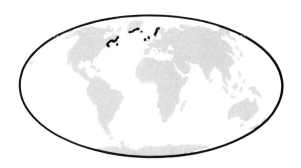

Peter J. Sharp

RAINTREE
STECK-VAUGHN
L I B R A R Y

Austin, Texas

CONTENTS

INTRODUCTION

High, craggy coasts, swept by wind and sea, the shrill cries of sea gulls and the soft calls of seals are images that immediately bring to mind the Atlantic Ocean. This ocean is a powerful barrier, keeping North American flora and fauna separated from those of Europe. But in a sense it is also a "bridge" for sea species. Quite often the same species live on both sides of this huge expanse of water.

The Atlantic Ocean has been sailed for the purposes of commerce and industry since the beginning of history. Today it is crossed in every direction by ships and planes, but the outcome of so much activity is not always positive. Some of this heavy traffic poses a threat to the future of ocean life, and even of humanity. On the other hand, intense interest in the Atlantic Ocean has given rise to new scientific theories on nature. It also provided a basis for the first steps toward nature conservation.

The history that deals with the increasing awareness of nature is long, but most recent developments date back to a

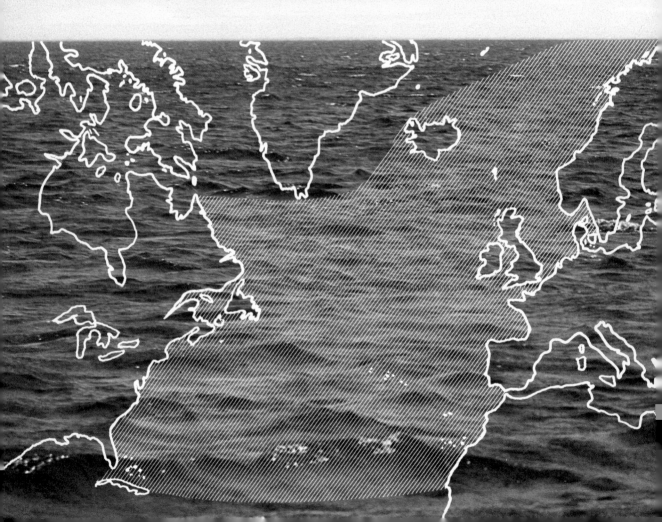

little over one hundred years ago. The role played by the English-speaking countries in this development cannot be forgotten. Almost all modern movements relating to the protection of endangered species, scenery, and environment originated with them. It should also be remembered that in those same countries many threats to nature exist. For example, the great numbers of whalers, fishermen, hunters, and adventurers thriving in these same areas have caused the extinction of the great auk and have brought many other species perilously close to a similar fate.

Not only the flow of water, but also the flow of ideas has influenced the Atlantic Ocean. While on both sides of the Atlantic Ocean nature has been heavily exploited, at the same time the ideological and philosophical basis for its protection has also been established. Of course, these concepts are neither perfect nor necessarily final. They represent, however, a step forward and will have implications for many years to come.

AN OVERVIEW

The Atlantic Ocean is the second largest ocean in the world. All in all, it covers an area of about 41 million square miles (106.9 million square kilometers), which is almost 24 percent of the entire water-covered surface of the world.

The Atlantic Ocean is much smaller than the Pacific Ocean (70 million sq. miles/180 million sq. km), and slightly larger than the Indian Ocean (29 million sq. miles/75 million sq. km).

Structure and Boundaries

The northern part of the Atlantic Ocean separates northern Europe and North Africa from North America. This is by far the best-known part of the ocean. Its irregular coastline is rich in islands.

To the west, the Atlantic Coast stretches from northern Labrador all the way to Florida. Its southern boundaries have traditionally been marked by a long stretch of islands (the West Indies) which surrounds the Caribbean Sea. To the east are the coastlines of Norway, the British Isles, France, Spain, Portugal, and Morocco. On both sides of the Atlantic, the northern coasts are very jagged, with abundant bays, estuaries, and islands of all sizes. Two of the largest islands are Newfoundland to the west, and the British Isles to the east. They are part of the continental shelves of North America and Europe, respectively.

Three large bays are found along the western coast: the Gulf of Saint Lawrence, the Bay of Fundy, and the Chesapeake Bay. In contrast, the only large bay found on the eastern coast is the Bay of Biscay. East of the British Isles, the North Sea covers part of the continental shelf. Until eight thousand years ago, when Great Britain was still connected to continental Europe, this was the largest bay in the North Atlantic.

Geographically speaking, the southern boundaries of the North Atlantic are marked by the equator. Climatically, however, it is more appropriate to set the southern limits along the course of the north-equatorial stream. This stream crosses the Atlantic from northern Africa to the West Indies.

To the northeast, a large underwater plateau running from Scotland to Iceland separates the Atlantic Ocean from the seas of the Arctic Circle. Part of this plateau rises above sea level, forming the Faeroe Islands. The stretch of underwater plateau between Scotland and the Faeroe Islands is less than 1,475 feet (450 meters) deep and is called the Wyville-Thomson Ridge. This ridge is a very effective bar-

Preceding page: The tail of a right whale protrudes from the water. This is the way it looks as the animal is about to dive. Whales, which were long hunted for their immense fat reserves, are among the species most affected by human's exploitation of ocean resources.

Opposite: The Atlantic coast can appear completely different in different places. There are high, sandy dunes midway down the European coast; jagged, rocky cliffs in the Scandinavian territories; beaches in Florida; and fjords in Labrador. In the picture are the cliffs of Slea Head, Ireland. The Blasket Islands are in the background. Ocean erosion adds to the sheer, rough look of the coast.

rier preventing the cold bottom waters of the Arctic from mixing with those of the North Atlantic. On the other hand, it allows warmer surface waters to flow from north to south. This ridge has a fundamental role in maintaining a temperate climate, almost always mild, in western Europe.

The Birth of the Atlantic Ocean

The outer part of the earth is composed of solid tectonic plates. The word *tectonic* refers to changes in the structure of the earth's surface. There, plates are 3 to 4 miles (5 to 7 km) thick beneath the ocean, and 12 to 43 miles (20 to 70 km) thick under the continents. They float on an inner, hot, semifluid layer, called the "mantle." The so-called continental plates are the parts of the plates that emerge from beneath the surface of the water. The movements of the plates are caused by basaltic magma, which flows out from the inner layer at the plates' edges. This magma cools down, adding more material to the earth's crust. It pushes the edges of the plates apart, causing mountain chains to rise and volcanoes to form. In order to make room for the new crust that is continually forming, the opposing edges of two plates overlap. One of the plates is forced to sink toward the inner layers of the earth where it heats up more and more, eventually melting and turning into magma. Part of this magma is pushed up to the surface again, flowing out through volcanic craters. Rows of volcanoes always mark subsidence

For many millions of years, the North American and Euro-Asiatic continental plates pushed against each other. They formed a continuous, huge stretch of dry land. In the illustration, the land appears as it probably was 180 to 225 million years ago. Due to the collision of the two plates, two huge mountain systems arose. Today, the Appalachians and the Caledonians are the remnants of these mountains. The Appalachian and Caledonian front ranges, as well as the areas where the mountains rose, are shown in color.

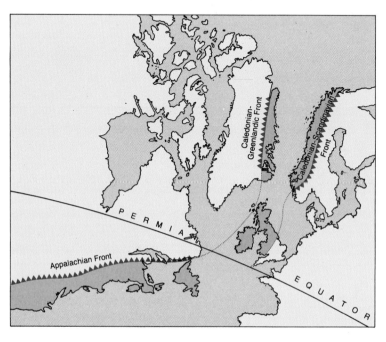

A picture captures the short but green summer on the Lofoten Islands. In the northernmost parts of the Atlantic Ocean, the mountains that rose during the Permian period were directly on the sea. They have been breaking down into numerous cliffs and small islands. This is due partially to ocean erosion and partially to the action of the Quaternary glaciers. The Lofoten Archipelago includes only a little of the over 150,000 islands, large and small, that are scattered along the Norwegian coast.

areas where plates have sunk along the edges of the plates.

The earth's plates have been moving continually for millions of years. They break apart, change their shape, and are reformed. As a result, new surface features are always appearing on the earth's crust. Throughout the geological ages, the changing mosaic of tectonic plates has been reflected in the continual reshaping of the continents which lay on top of them. During the long history of the earth, the continental masses have most certainly broken apart and merged again in a different way more than once.

In the last 500 to 600 million years, the North American and Euro-Asiatic plates have collided and broken apart twice. Each collision was followed by the rise of mountains along the plates' edges. What remains of these mountains is called the "Appalachian Front" in North America. On the British Isles and along the coasts of Norway and Greenland, it is called the "Caledonian Front."

The North Atlantic Ocean, as it is today, started forming about 159 million years ago. At that time, new cracks opened up along the edges of the North American and Euro-Asiatic plates. The widening of the ocean bottom between the plates' edges has been slow by human standards, but very fast in geological terms. Today, the Atlantic Ocean widens by 2 inches (5 centimeters) each year. This means that the crossing to America, on the same route that Columbus followed, is already 82 feet (25 m) longer.

The melted rock flows out through the earth's crust along a north-south rift in the middle of the Atlantic Ocean. Immense underwater mountain chains are created on each side of the rift. Several parallel mountain chains have risen in this way, and the farther they are from the central rift, the older they are. This system of underwater mountain chains is called the Mid-Atlantic Ridge.

Usually, the Mid-Atlantic Ridge is 3,281 to 6,562 feet (1,000 to 2,000 m) below the surface of the ocean, but here and there volcanic islands may emerge. The largest of these is Iceland, where the process of the parting of the plates can still be clearly seen. Molten rock flows from a crack which crosses the entire island. Continuous eruptions form numerous craters and wide lava fields. If the molten rock cannot force its way out, it will instead heat up the overlying rock layers. This creates hundreds of hot springs and spectacular geysers. Due to the continual lava flows, the surface of Iceland grows a few inches each year.

The Gulf Stream

The surface currents of the North Atlantic move clockwise in a wide circle. A large side current detaches from this circle and heads northeast, toward the Arctic Ocean. Most of these ocean currents are rather slow, moving at about 0.6 miles (1 km) per hour. The Gulf Stream, however, moves at over 5 miles (9 km) per hour.

The circle of ocean currents approximately matches the pattern of the prevailing winds. These winds actually cause the currents to swirl. The winds are created when the sun's rays heat up the air in the equatorial regions, making the air lighter. This hot air tends to rise and is replaced by cooler air coming from both the north and the south. Due to the rotation of the earth, the winds are shifted laterally. The North-Equatorial and South-Equatorial Currents, which are formed as a result of this process, head north toward the Caribbean Sea. There these currents become trapped be-

Iceland, which has risen atop the Mid-Atlantic Ridge, is the largest volcanic island in the world. Intense eruptive phenomena occur along a band that crosses the entire island. About 10 percent of the territory is covered by lava flows that are less than ten thousand years old. A recent, spectacular eruption caused the formation of Surtsey Island in 1963. In 1973, another eruption on nearby Heimaey Island caused the destruction of the main fishing harbor in Iceland, Vestmannaeyjar.

The surface waters of the Atlantic Ocean are not still. They move in a circle in a clockwise direction, following the course of the prevailing winds. The winds, in turn, are caused by the earth's rotation and by the Coriolis forces. This causes tropical, warm waters to move northeast. They reach the coasts of Europe all the way up to the northernmost regions of Norway. The warm Gulf Stream does not affect the coast of North America. It is influenced by a cold current coming from the Arctic. This current extends all the way to the Caribbean Sea. For this reason, there are rich, coastal heaths along the European coast, while at the same latitude in Labrador, barren tundra stretches face the ocean.

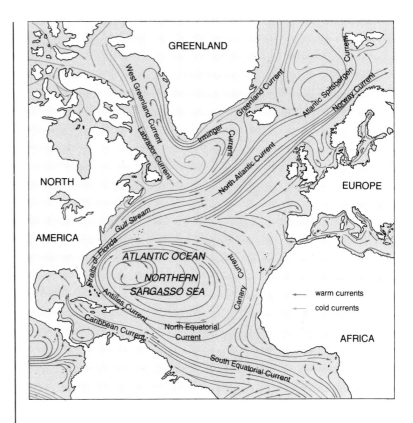

tween the coast of the American continent and the islands parallel to it. The principal flow out of this "Caribbean trap" is through the Straits of Florida. This is a stretch of open sea, about 50 miles (80 km) wide, between Florida and Cuba. The waters flow out from the Caribbean Sea at a rate of 10 cubic miles (40 cubic km) per hour. This "river" is 1,312 feet (400 m) deep and is called the "Florida Current." The current gains speed due to the winds and the Coriolis effect (forces generated by the earth's rotation). It then merges with the circular current of the Atlantic. Flowing north off the eastern coasts of the United States, it next becomes part of the Gulf Stream. The warm waters of the Gulf Stream then move through much colder waters. This, plus the fact that the prevailing winds blow from land to sea, accounts for the fact that the stream does not in any way mitigate the cold winter climate of the eastern United States.

Off the coast of Newfoundland, the Gulf Stream is deflected east by various factors. Some of these are the prevailing winds, the Coriolis effect, and certain changes in the ocean bottom. West of Newfoundland, in the Grand Banks area, the Gulf Stream meets with the cold waters of

Pictured is Cape Cod in Massachusetts. The action of constant currents often creates sand tongues that jut out into the open sea. They form magnificent, natural scenery.

the Labrador Current, which flows from north to south. As a result, the warm air over the Gulf Stream mingles with the cold air over the Labrador Current, and most of the humidity in the air condenses into thick fog. Moreover, the Labrador Current carries many icebergs from the Arctic Ocean with it. One of these icebergs, invisible until the last moment because of fog, caused the sinking of the British steamer, *Titanic,* in 1912.

On the last part of its route east, the Gulf Stream slows down and splits into several branches. One of them continues moving clockwise, maintaining the circulation of the Atlantic waters and forming the slow Canaries Current.

The waters of this branch are colder than the waters it

flows through off northern Africa. This causes large fog-banks to be formed. The main flow of this current called the "North Atlantic Drift," continues to move northeast. It laps the shores of northwestern Europe and heads up to the threshold of the Arctic Ocean. The warm waters of the drift keep the coasts of northern Norway free of ice and at the same time heat up the cold air coming down from the north. Because of this current, the climate of northern Europe is maritime and humid, with mild winters and cool summers. This is the so-called Atlantic climate, much milder than the climate along the American coast at the same latitude.

The Tides

A notable feature of the Atlantic shores is the size of the tides. Because the mass of water in the Atlantic Ocean is so huge, it is greatly affected by the gravitational attraction of the moon and sun, as well as by the centrifugal forces resulting from the earth's rotation. These forces interact, and twice a day cause the rising and falling of tides. The size of the tides varies periodically according to the specific position of the earth, moon, and sun.

Certain characteristics such as local currents, the shape of the coast, etc. also affect the tide levels. The highest tides occur in the Bay of Fundy in Canada and have a range of 50 feet (15 m) or more. On the other hand, at Cape Cod the tide range is only 3 feet (1 m). Around the British Isles, the tides are highest in the Bristol Channel. There, a 40 foot (12 m) difference between low and high tide occurs. On the other hand, the tidal range along the coasts of the English Channel is only 6 feet (2 m).

Various Kinds of Coasts

The Atlantic coasts, like those of the other oceans, are highly varied. There are vast sandy and/or pebbly beaches, with stones of varying sizes. Also found are rocky cliffs, some with gentle slopes, others with very steep ones. Many beaches are completely exposed to the action of the waves. Pounding surf exerts an average pressure of 1,986 pounds per square foot (9,700 kilograms per square meter). During the most violent storms, this crushing pressure can average 6,144 pounds per square foot (30,000 kg/sq. m). The waves carve the softer sedimentary rocks into twisted shapes. Eventually only the hardest rocks are left, forming vertical walls, isolated cliffs and promontories, which are high points of land or rock projecting into a body of water.

ROCKY COASTS

The rocky coasts of the Atlantic Ocean are often covered by seaweed and lichens. Lichens are primitive plants formed by the association of blue-green algae with fungi. They create horizontal layers at many levels. This "zonation" reflects the different tolerance level of each species to immersion in water, light, and wave motion. The "splash" zone is an area where only splashes of water reach. This is a transition zone between marine and terrestrial habitats. It is the most colorful zone because it is inhabited by numerous species of yellow, orange, and gray lichens. A further touch of color is added by some flowering plants which tolerate the high salinity.

Seaweed

The lower limit of the splash zone is marked by a black belt. At first glance, this may seem to have been created by pollution caused by people. It is actually a colony of blue-green algae of the genus *Calothrix* or a colony of black lichen of the genus *Verrucaria*. This black belt is, in fact, part of the marine habitat proper because periodic immersion during high tide is essential to its survival.

Below the black belt, plant life is dominated by a succession of numerous species of brown seaweed, that extends downward below the low-tide limit. Unlike terrestrial plants, seaweeds do not have roots, but "hook" themselves to the rocks instead. Like terrestrial plants, they use the sunlight to produce complex sugars through the process of photosynthesis.

The largest brown seaweeds, the kelps, grow on the rocks of the sub-littoral zone. The littoral zone is the coastal region, extending between the high and low watermarks. In this zone, the seaweeds form thick forests which can be 6 to 10 feet (2 to 3 m) high. Their stalks correspond to a plant's trunk and their wide blades correspond to a plant's leaves. They form an especially good habitat for many species of animals and other plants. On the more exposed coasts, one of the most common species is the horsetail kelp. The common southern kelp is most often found along the sheltered coasts.

Green and red seaweeds also grow in horizontal belts, although the belts are not as clearly defined as with the brown seaweeds. The green seaweeds contain a green pigment, chlorophyll, and are common on the high and middle levels of the coast. The red seaweeds contain a red pigment, phycoerythrin. These plants are more suited than the green

Opposite: A thick mat of horsetail kelp is seen. This seaweed grows from the low-tide line to depths of 66 to 98 feet (20 to 30 m). It is among the largest of brown seaweeds. In the higher zones of the shore, smaller species usually take its place. Among these are the rockweed and the knotted wrack. Both have round air bladders that cause their leaves to float on the surface during high tide.

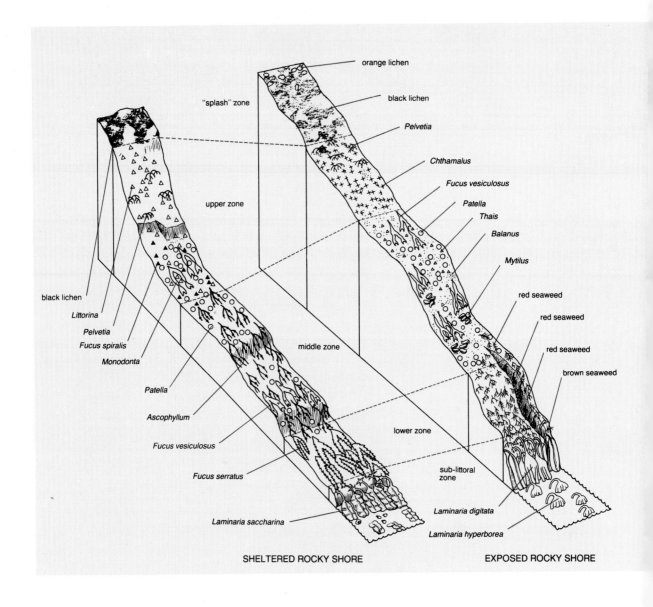

orange lichen

black lichen

Pelvetia

Chthamalus

Fucus vesiculosus

Patella

Thais

Balanus

Mytilus

red seaweed

red seaweed

red seaweed

brown seaweed

"splash" zone

upper zone

middle zone

lower zone

sub-littoral zone

black lichen

Littorina

Pelvetia

Fucus spiralis

Monodonta

Patella

Ascophyllum

Fucus vesiculosus

Fucus serratus

Laminaria saccharina

Laminaria digitata

Laminaria hyperborea

SHELTERED ROCKY SHORE

EXPOSED ROCKY SHORE

The distribution of animal and plant life in the various zones of the rocky shores off the North American coast is determined by the resistance of the different organisms to air exposure. The "splash" zone is never flooded by the ocean waters. The upper zone is flooded only by the highest tides. The lower zone emerges from the water only during the lowest tides. The size of the different zones, as well as the number of species, varies according to whether the shore is sheltered or exposed. The species in the drawing are typical of the British coasts.

for using dim light in the photosynthesis process which converts light into energy.

The Barnacles

It is not only seaweeds and lichens that form horizontal belts along the rocky coasts. Some animals typical of these environments also tend to form bands which reflect their varying degrees of tolerance to air exposure. Barnacle belts, which are especially evident on the most exposed coasts, look like concrete. The primitive barnacle shell consists of four or five calcareous (containing limestone or calcium

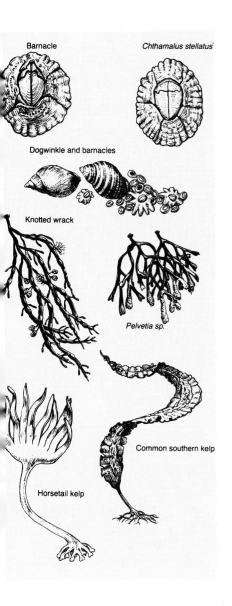

Barnacle

Chthamalus stellatus

Dogwinkle and barnacles

Knotted wrack

Pelvetia sp.

Horsetail kelp

Common southern kelp

carbonate) plates which form a conical shape. The central opening is covered by a protective trap door divided into four segments. When the tide rises, the trap door opens. The feathery, modified legs called "cirri" of these small animals extend outward. The cirri are well suited for filtering the water and grasping microscopic food particles which are then pulled inside. The *Chthamalus stellatus,* with a six-plate shell, and the northern rock barnacle are among the most common species in the Atlantic Ocean.

Periwinkles and Limpets

Both periwinkles and limpets belong to a large class of mollusks known as "gastropods." Most members of this group, which includes snails, have a single, coiled shell or none at all. Periwinkles are among the most common sea snails which dwell on the rocky coasts.

Various species have developed different adaptations which permit them to occupy specific shore zones and feed on the carpets of seaweeds. The tiniest periwinkle of the European shores, *Littorina neritoides,* is 0.2 inches (5 millimeters) long. It has adapted to life on the upper level of the shore, mainly in the splash zone, where it hides deep in rock cracks. Its respiratory chamber is modified, so that it can breathe air. It can also turn its nitrogenous wastes into a non-toxic substance, urea, like many land animals do. When it is time to lay its eggs, however, this snail must go back to the ocean.

Among all the gastropods living on the rocky shores, the limpet is best adapted to withstand the violence of the waves. First its conical shell can withstand the impact of the surf. Second, its sucker-like foot allows it to stick to the rocks. This second feature almost makes it impossible to displace the limpet. Exactly how the animals achieve such a powerful grip is unknown. It is possible that an adhesive substance is secreted from various glands on the foot.

Limpets feed mainly on microscopic algae, which they scrape from the rock surface with a specialized tongue. This scraping action leaves a distinctive pattern on the softer rocks, and prevents the growth of larger algae. Most of the limpets discovered along the North Atlantic coasts are found in Europe. In the United States they are less common.

Lobsters and Crabs

The most well-known crustaceans of the rocky shores are also the largest of the family. These are the lobsters and

The European lobster, *Palinurus vulgaris*, is quite closely related to the crab. Unlike the crab, it has an elongated abdomen. Because of their different shape, lobsters can move around more easily and prey upon mobile animals, such as sea urchins.

the crabs. Among the lobsters, three species receive the most attention. They are the European lobster, the spiny lobster, and the northern lobster. The spiny and the northern are both found in America. The delicacy of lobster meat has certainly not helped the survival of these species. Excessive fishing, together with a progressive cooling of the Atlantic waters, has brought the lobster fishing industry to the verge of extinction.

Lobsters are solitary, aggressive animals that live in deep waters off the shore. At night they hunt for sea urchins, mollusks, and worms. During the day they stay hidden in the kelp forests or in rock cracks.

One of the most common species of crabs along the rocky shores is the green crab. It is a European species, but it has been introduced in America. It is a voracious predator, hunting and killing worms and mollusks. In some regions, this crab can cause serious damage to commercial clam cultures, especially to those of the soft-shelled clam. Other crabs found along the American shores are the rock crab and the common spider crab. To the south, the green crab is gradually replaced by the blue crab. This is an important commercial species as each year 900 to 3,600 tons of blue crab are harvested.

The Starfish

Starfish are important predators. They have a specialized water-vascular system, which operates a great many tube feet. Each tube foot has a sucker at its end. The feet move due to variations in the water pressure inside them. These variations are created by the water-vascular system which pumps water in and out of the feet. Starfish move about in this way. The combined action of the tube feet is so effective that these animals can climb vertical walls or open the shell of a clam.

Brittle starfish are often found hidden under rocks or pebbles in the lower shore zone. They have long, flexible arms which they use to crawl on the sea floor with snake-like movements. They feed on bristle worms, small crustaceans, and debris. Their tube feet are much smaller.

The invertebrates which live in the lower shore zone are prey to predator vertebrates, such as fish and birds, and also to a great many invertebrates, such as squid, cuttlefish, and octopus.

The bright coloration of the green crab is perfect camouflage among the seaweeds. This species is common on both European and American Atlantic shores. It is the most voracious predator of sedentary animals that live attached to the sea floor.

21

SANDY BEACHES

The high-tide line is easily recognized on sandy beaches. It is marked by a band of rotting seaweed and other organic material. Seashells, the remains of sea urchins and crabs, conch egg sacs, sponges, and jelly clumps (jellyfish remains) are found here. This is the habitat of the beach flea, a tiny animal only 0.2 inches (5 mm) long. These amphibious crustaceans resemble shrimp and live in holes dug in the sand. These holes are often dug on the most exposed beaches. Their hideaways are kept sheltered and wet by the rotting seaweed that accumulates on top of them. When the seaweed is removed, swarms of beach fleas hop away in every direction. There are several different species. Each is adapted to life in a particular zone above the low-tide line. When the tide rises, they emerge from their shelters and follow the tidal wave. They then feed on the animal and plant debris carried in by the water.

Digging Mollusks and Tube-worms

On more sheltered beaches, beach fleas are less numerous. Here the most common animals are digging bivalves and bristle worms. Many of these animals feed on organic particles carried by the water. They catch this food with their specialized filtering devices or sticky tentacles. Other animals feed on the surface of the sand. They swallow tiny particles deposited on the sand, or they swallow the sand entirely and retain that which is edible. The debris-eaters tend to be more common where sand mixes with silt (earthy material that settles to the bottom of bodies of water). This occurs especially in river estuaries where an arm of the sea meets the lower end of a river.

Bivalves are animals, such as clams, that have two-part, hinged shells. The most common bivalves which dig shallow holes in the sand of American shores are the gem shell, the surf clam, the Morton's egg cockle, the common razor clam, and the hard-shelled clam. The gem shell is the main food for shrimp, worms, crabs, and diving ducks. The surf clam is the favorite prey of gulls. The birds drop the clams repeatedly from great heights until the shell breaks open.

Many species of sedentary tube-worms are found in the lower zones of sandy beaches. These worms live in their tubes, which they build with sand and a sticky secretion or mucus. Fan worms (Sabella pavonina) are typical of filtering organisms. The head of this worm has a fan of striped, feathery tentacles. This gives it the appearance of a colorful flower. When the fan worm is under the water, its tentacle

Opposite: A starfish is an astonishing predator. It is at ease both on sandy shores and on rocky shores. Its movements are slow, but it is exceptionally strong. It can easily open the most tightly-closed bivalve shells. It digests the edible parts of its prey directly from the shell, reaching in with its extensible stomach. This stomach extends from the base of its arms at the point where they merge to form the central disk. When the flesh of the prey has become liquid, the starfish swallows it. Pictured is a red asterias.

23

Right: The crown of feathery tentacles that *Sabella pavoniana* flutters in the water is a filtering device. It traps microorganisms and food particles that are suspended in the water. This worm is a distant relative of the earthworm. It is sedentary and lives inside a tube. The tube is formed from a liquid that the body secretes that soon hardens.

Opposite: Some animals of the sandy beaches of northern Europe are *(from top to bottom):* the frail skeleton of the sea urchin; the same species buried in the sand; the moon snail; the crustaceans *Corystes cassivelaunus;* and *Crangon vulgaris;* and the fish *Ammodytes tobianus.* This fish is called the sand eel because of its slender body and numerous vertebrae.

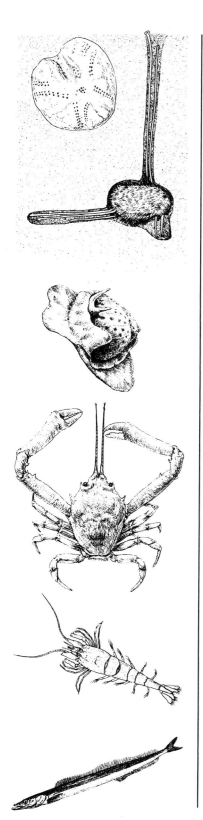

crown emerges from the tube. The feathery cilia flutter and come together over the center. This traps particles of food. While the worm is feeding, it can sense even the slightest disturbance. It may be only a shadow passing over or a vibration. Whatever the cause, the animal immediately responds to such stimuli by retreating into its tube.

The Predators

The debris-eaters and the particle-eaters are the favorite prey of many digging animals. These predator animals include bristle worms, starfish, conchs, shrimp, crabs, and sand lances. The clam worm is one of the longest predator worms, reaching up to 39 inches (100 cm). It has a beautiful opalescent green or coppery brown coloration. The digging starfish belongs to the genus *Astropecten* and is called a margined starfish. It feeds on small bivalves, sponges, and crustaceans, which it swallows in one gulp.

The European predator snail is closely related to the American moon shell and lives just below the sandy surface. It laboriously pushes its way around with its large, two-lobed foot, in search of its prey, the small bivalves. When it finds a clam, it wraps it in its foot, drills a hole in the shell, and sucks out the soft contents. These sea snails lay their eggs inside a sandy ring. They secrete a mucus that hardens the ring and then they wrap it around themselves. These sand rings are often washed ashore by waves.

Several species of shrimp belonging to the genus *Crangon* live in the sand. These sand shrimp stay hidden during the day with only their eyes and antennae showing above the sand. Sometimes they can be found above the low-tide line, but usually they spend their entire lives under the water. They feed on organic debris, small worms, and crustaceans.

Sand lances are often found in large numbers in the shallow waters of sandy bays. They feed on zooplankton, the tiny animal members of the plankton community. They also feed on worms and crustaceans. These fish are 5 to 6 inches (12.5 to 15 cm) long and look somewhat like eels, although they are not related.

These fish are fast and powerful diggers. If chased by a predator or when the tide retreats, lances can completely bury themselves in the sand, using their spoon-shaped jaws to dig. They form an important part of the diets of many larger fish, such as cod, mackerel, and salmon and also of seabirds such as the puffins. Today, these fish are ground

into fish meal, which is used as both fertilizer and animal food. If this activity is not controlled, the decrease of the sand lance population might threaten the survival of those species that depend upon it.

Mussels and Oysters

Mussels and oysters are bivalves that also filter their food from the water. Unlike many related species, however, they do not protect themselves by digging holes in the sand. Both mussels and oysters are edible and are used commercially all along the Atlantic Coast.

Mussels live in great numbers in the low- or middle-shore zone. They are firmly attached to rocks, boulders, pilings, dock foundations, and other supports. They are especially common on muddy bottoms. There they grow in layers, and eventually form actual heaps. The mussel can moor itself to any hard surface with threads called "byssus" that are produced by a gland in the foot. These threads are elastic and allow the mussel to sway with the current, without resisting the action of the flow of water. If the

The horseshoe crab is an extraordinary example of a living fossil. It has lived along the coast of North America for over 200 million years without undergoing any major evolutionary changes. This crab finds its food in the mud or in the sand.

26

Many species of bivalve mollusks live buried in the sandy bottoms of the North Atlantic. *From left to right:* Baltic macoma, soft-shelled clam, gem shell, quahog or hard-shelled clam, tellin, razor clam. All of these species have a shell with noticeable, concentric growth ridges. They also have a strong, expansible foot with which they can dig into the sand. Some of these species can bury themselves in the bottom so quickly that it is practically impossible to catch them. These mollusks have two siphons that can be extended all the way to the surface. One of them draws in water loaded with oxygen and suspended food particles. The other flushes out filtered water and droppings. Tellins, unlike other bivalves, can feed on the debris that accumulates on the sea floor. They draw it in with their inhaling siphons.

environmental conditions turn adverse, the mussel can break loose and move to a better location on its foot.

Some people feel oysters are even more delicious than mussels. American oysters live on the shore just below the low-tide line where they form large banks. The most important bank is in Chesapeake Bay and is commercially exploited. The European oyster requires warmer, saltier waters than its American relative.

The Horseshoe Crab

On the eastern coasts of North America lives a very peculiar animal. At first sight, it vaguely resembles the extinct trilobites which were Paleozoic era marine animals. This animal is the horseshoe crab. As an arthropod, it is related to spiders and scorpions. It has remained unchanged for over 200 million years. On its upper side, the horseshoe crab is covered by a thick, horny armor. It has eight legs and a long spike-like tail, rigid and pointed.

In spring, the horseshoe crabs gather in large numbers to lay their eggs during high tide. The females dig their nests in the sand and lay thousands of eggs for the males to fertilize. The receding tidal flow covers the nests with sand and washes some of the adults back to sea.

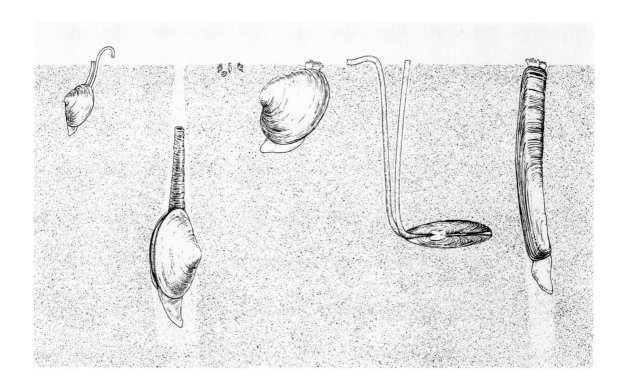

ESTUARIES

Estuaries are places of silt expanses and brackish swamps. They may sound like dull and unappealing environments but are, in fact, home to very complex and unique animal communities. The daily tides continually bring nutrients to the silt flats. This adds to the debris carried by ocean waves and by the river. The tides rise and fall twice a day, allowing a complete mixing of nutrients. If the water is not too murky, large quantities of phytoplankton (the plant members of the plankton community) colonize the silt surface and the upper layers. If the tidal currents are not too strong, vast expanses of green seaweed develop due to the nutrient-rich waters. Phytoplankton, seaweed, debris from rotting seaweed and swamp vegetation, and all the material carried by the river form plant matter. This plant matter is the basis for many food chains.

Fresh Waters and Salt Waters

In the estuaries, the water salinity, which is the amount of salt in a solution, varies continually. This is because the ocean water carried by the tide meets and mingles with fresh water from the river. The degree of mingling of fresh and sea waters varies in each estuary and depends upon the interaction of two factors. The first factor is the speed of the fresh water flow. The second is the intensity of the tidal currents. Moreover, the mingling of waters can occur in different zones along the estuary, depending on the stage of the tide. When fresh water mingles with salt water, the tiniest silt particles dissolved in the water attract one another. They clump together in a process called "flocculation." They then become heavier and sink to the bottom. There they form a layer of gelatin-like silt which covers all underwater surfaces.

Most of the animal and plant species, both marine and freshwater, cannot tolerate the continuous variations in salinity. Barnacles and starfish, for example, never venture deep into the estuaries, because exposure to fresh water quickly kills them. The deadly effect of fresh water on barnacles has long been taken advantage of by sailors. They have had to deal with the continuous accumulation of barnacles on the hulls of their ships. Mooring ships in fresh water for a week is enough to wipe out these crustaceans. Likewise, starfish cannot tolerate fresh water. So oysters and mussels, the principal prey of starfish, are abundant in the brackish waters of the estuaries. They live off the starfish who find their way into the "deadly" fresh water.

Opposite: Swamps form marine waters on Texel Island in Holland. The brackish, swampy flats that form near estuaries are environments that teem with life. These areas offer shelter to complex communities of invertebrates, together with the fish that prey on them. During migration periods, these environments are crowded with huge flocks of birds, mainly ducks and shorebirds. Many of the birds stay for the winter.

29

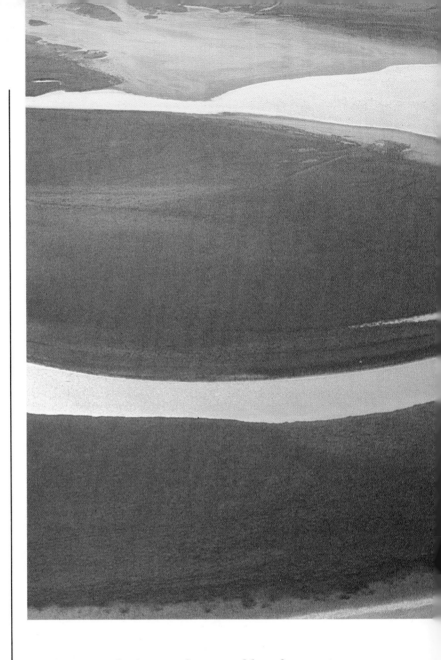

A labyrinth of channels cuts through an eelgrass prairie. Eelgrass is one of the few flowering plants to thrive in salt water. It anchors to the bottom by means of rhizoms (horizontal, underground plant stems), each of which acts as the base for several stalks. These plants form intricate prairies where many small animals find food and shelter.

Species which can tolerate sudden changes in estuary salinity are referred to as "euryhaline." Their numbers are small when compared to the saltwater or freshwater species. However, their population size can be quite large. The small number of euryhaline species is explained by the harsh environment that they must survive in. Another contributing factor is the limited numbers of habitats that exist in the estuary. The main estuary habitat is the silt expanse.

The Eelgrass Communities

In the lower zones of the estuaries and in shallow bays all along the Atlantic Coast, eelgrass forms wide, under-

water prairies. This marine seed plant grows below the low-tide line at the point where light no longer reaches the bottom. It is firmly anchored in the sand. Eelgrass can tolerate a reduction in salinity, down to a value of 0.1 percent. But it is incapable of living in less salty waters. For this reason, it cannot colonize the higher zones of the estuary.

Eelgrass prairies play an important role in estuary ecology. They are more productive than a wheat or hay field and offer food and shelter to many animal communities. Their roots stabilize the recently deposited sediments. This forms a solid base for other microorganisms to develop. Their leaves trap the sediments. This entire process even-

31

Odostome

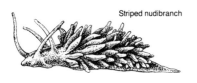

Striped nudibranch

Idotea baltica

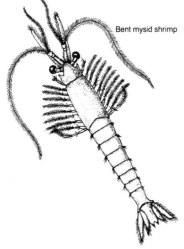

Bent mysid shrimp

The invertebrates of the eelgrass prairies

tually forms silt banks that often evolve into brackish swamps.

The thicket of leaves in the eelgrass prairies supports a great many plants and sedentary invertebrates. Sometimes the mass of these "guests" can equal that of the "host" plants. Close examination of an eelgrass leaf reveals epifauna and epiphytes. These are animals and plants respectively, that use other plants as support. They are distributed on the leaf in clearly defined zones. The lower part of the leaf is the newest. It is covered by unicellular plants called "diatoms." Higher up are found red and green seaweeds. These epiphytic algae are a source of food. They are softer than eelgrass and more easily digested by both the sedentary and mobile animals that feed on them. Among the sedentary animals are hydroid worms, sponges, sea anemones, and bryozoans. Included with the freely moving animals are green bonellia, flatworms, isopods, and amphipods. Numerous species of amphipods, which are small crustaceans such as beach fleas, use the debris to build protective tubes. These tubes form a soft mat around the base of the eelgrass. Several species of sea snails use the eelgrass leaves.

Shell-less mollusks are also common on the eelgrass. Some of these feed on algae, while others are carnivores. One type of carnivore is the striped nudibranch. It lives in North America and feeds on hydroids which are invertebrates such as jellyfish.

Eelgrass prairies also attract crustaceans such as the tiny mysid shrimp. These animals grow from 0.4 to 0.8 inches (1 to 2 cm) long, and hang vertically from grass stems. They camouflage themselves perfectly by being able to change color quickly. While almost transparent in clear water, they become gray-brown in murky water. Crabs are also common in this environment. The young use the eelgrass as a nursery, while the adults move about looking for food. The prairies later serve as shelter after the crabs cast off their shells. Among the most common fish are the sea horse and the needlefish. Both are difficult to spot in the grass because they imitate the movement of plants with their bodies. The females lay their eggs in an incubation sac within the male's body. This sac is formed by two elongated folds along the belly of the fish.

Silt Stretches

Silt gradually accumulates inside the estuaries. Between low and high tide, the silt remains exposed. Wide

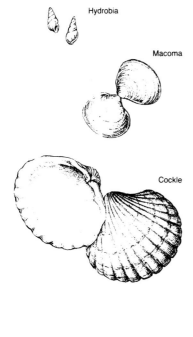

Hydrobia

Macoma

Cockle

Scrobicularia sp.

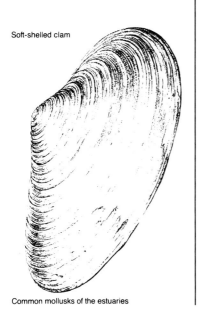

Soft-shelled clam

Common mollusks of the estuaries

expanses of it are formed. Eelgrass cannot grow in these environments because it cannot tolerate the constant immersion. Seaweed and bacteria, however, abound here. The most important seaweeds are the hollow weeds of the order *Enteromorpha,* which are a bright green color, and the sea lettuce. Many small animals live beneath the surface of the silt. In this way they can escape predators and find protection from currents and waves. The most common animals are the round parasitic worms, or nematodes, which are less than 0.07 inches (2 mm) long. Life in the mud creates some problems that do not exist for the creatures that live in the sandy bottoms. For example, since mud is not as porous as sand, water circulation is hindered. Because of this, the supply of oxygen in the water is restricted. The digging animals that breathe through their skin cannot survive in the silt. Only the animals that have special adaptations for acquiring their oxygen supply can live in such environments. The filtering mollusks do not dwell in the silt stretches because their filtering devices clog quickly.

The most numerous sea snail in the silt expanses is the swamp hydrobia, which is about as large as a kernel of wheat. The swamp hydrobia feeds on seaweed, especially sea lettuce and hollow green weeds, and on bacteria. Other estuary mollusks, unlike the swamp hydrobia, spend all their lives buried in the mud. The Baltic macoma, for example, lives just beneath the surface. It feeds by drawing in algae and organic debris with its inhalant siphon. This siphon is long and moves in a snake-like way along the bottom. The soft-shelled clam, an American species introduced into Europe, buries itself deep in the sandy mud, going down to a depth of 20 inches (50 cm). Another common bivalve of the estuaries is the cockle. The most common European species, *Cardium edule,* does not usually bury itself in the bottom and lives only where estuary mud is mixed with sand.

Among the digging animals, another very common species is the amphipod *Corophium volutator.* During hot, sunny days, silt stretches teem with these crustaceans. In the Firth of Tay in Scotland, over 2,800 individuals have been recorded in a square foot. Each one of these minute animals lives in a U-shaped tunnel. It creates a water current through the tunnel so that it can obtain oxygen and food particles from the flowing water.

Many species of worms also live in the silt expanses. The most well known are the clam worm and the lugworm.

The splendid blossoms of the sea lavender appear as swamps begin to fill with soil. When this happens, the number and diversity of plant species increase. This picture was taken in Norfolk, a county in southeastern England that faces the North Sea.

Both are used as bait by fishermen. These worms belong to the same bristle worm group, but their feeding patterns are quite different. The lugworm is a debris-eater and lives on the bottom in deep U-shaped burrows. It draws in water through a rear opening and swallows sand from the surface through a front opening. After feeding on the organic particles, the worm expels the sand through the rear. The clam worm, on the other hand, is a voracious predator that feeds on invertebrates. It seizes its prey in its powerful, black, horny jaws, which are a part of its expandable mouth.

Brackish Swamps

As a result of sediment accumulation, silt flats gradually rise. Eventually, some terrestrial plants begin to colonize the flats. The most common colonizing species are the glasswort and the marsh grass. The glasswort is a small, bushy plant. It removes salt from seawater and stores fresh water in its succulent stems and scaly leaves. It is an annual species and only its seeds survive during the winter. It is very common in the European brackish marshes. In America, it is less common and found mainly on recently formed sandy stretches where the terrain is often trampled upon.

On the North American Atlantic Coast, the main colonizing species is the marsh grass. Unlike the glasswort, this marsh grass manages to grow on very soft silt. It spreads rapidly, forming a dense network of underground stems, or rhizomes. A fully grown plant is 3 to 6 feet (1 to 2 m) tall and has stiff leaves. The first settlers of North America used it to cover the roofs of their houses. The marsh grass does well in saltwater. It is able to separate the salt from the water that it sucks in with its roots. The discarded salt is expelled through the leaves. There it accumulates, forming white patches as it dries. These patches are typical of the species. In 1870, the American marsh grass was introduced into Great Britain. It crossbred with the local, less vigorous species, *Spartina maritima*. The new hybrid species (resulting from the crossbreeding) is *Spartina townsendii*. It grows so fast that it hinders the growth of other swamp species. As a result, the amount of diversity in the brackish swamp habitat is reduced. The spread of this hybrid species has often been encouraged by certain individuals because it helps to drain marshes. The unfortunate consequence of this is that it seriously limits the availability of swamps as habitats for wildlife.

SHOREBIRDS AND WATER BIRDS

The large estuaries and ocean bays are perfect environments for a great many shorebirds. Some winter there. Others stop during their spring migrations toward the Arctic where they reproduce. Due to migration, the number of shorebirds found on the estuaries varies with the seasons. Numbers are low in late spring and summer when the birds reproduce. They are high in early spring and fall in the middle of the migratory period.

Most shorebirds have a dull, brownish, winter plumage when they stop in these regions. This makes them difficult to identify. The mating plumage, on the other hand, is much brighter. Contrasting black-and-white patterns alternate with various shades of brown. The birds have this coloration as they are migrating toward their mating sites and when they return.

Usually, the winter climate of the Atlantic Coast north of Cape Cod is too cold for shorebirds. Therefore, they head to the brackish swamps and estuaries more to the south. The climate of the British Isles, on the other hand, is mild enough to allow most of the shorebirds migrating toward the western coasts of Europe to stop and winter. A small number of Atlantic shorebirds live there year round, but they may migrate farther inland to their reproduction sites.

The Oystercatchers

The oystercatchers are easy to distinguish from other shorebirds. Each bird has a showy black-and-white plumage, pink legs, and a red bill. The American species is colored brown on its back and wings, while the European species is black in those same spots. In spite of its name, the oystercatcher feeds mainly on mussels, limpets, cockles, and crabs. In southern Wales, the oystercatcher's preference for cockles has put it in competition with the local fishermen who harvest this mollusk. As a result, these birds were heavily hunted during the 1970s. On the British Isles, the oystercatchers are year-round inhabitants and will reproduce there. During the winter months, their numbers are increased by the arrival of flocks from northern Europe. The American oystercatcher can be found south of Cape Cod but is beginning to nest in northern regions.

The Plovers

Among the shorebirds, the plover group is one of the most important. Usually these birds have short legs and a contrasting coloration. The most common plovers winter-

Opposite: From autumn to spring, the ocean shores are visited by flocks of many species of shorebirds that feed on invertebrates buried in the sand. The turnstone is not one of the most common species, but its brightly-colored plumage is unmistakable. With its bill, it turns over rocks, seaweed, and seashells scattered on the beach to find its food.

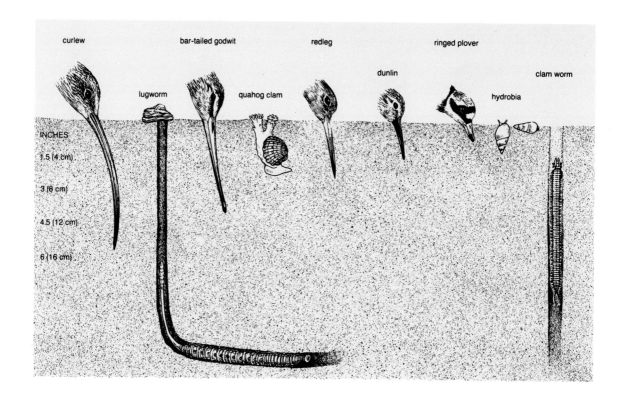

The image has the following labels: curlew, bar-tailed godwit, redleg, ringed plover, dunlin, clam worm, lugworm, quahog clam, hydrobia, INCHES, 1.5 (4 cm), 3 (8 cm), 4.5 (12 cm), 6 (16 cm)

The prey of shorebirds depends on the length of their bills. Birds like the ringed plover can only feed on the small organisms that live close to the surface. The curlew and the bar-tailed godwit can easily reach the deepest burrowing worms.

ing in the European estuaries are the black-bellied plover, the golden plover, and the ringed plover. The ringed plover reproduces both in the Arctic and along the British coasts. In America, the semipalmated plover is the most common variety. This bird gets its name from the fact that its toes are joined only part way down by a web. Another American species, the piping plover, is one of the few shorebirds that regularly nests along the eastern coast of the United States. The feeding pattern of plovers is distinctive and makes them easily recognizable. They alternate swift sprints and quick pecks with periods of complete stillness. Plovers have relatively short bills. They feed mainly on invertebrates that live in the upper sandy layers or on mud flats.

Sandpipers and Turnstones

Tiny shorebirds of the sandpiper group winter along both sides of the North Atlantic. These birds are particularly gregarious, both feeding and resting in groups. Their dull winter plumage makes them hard to notice from a distance. The dunlin is the only species whose reproductive area extends from the Arctic to the British Islands and Scandinavia. Another sandpiper, the knot, is larger and bulkier than

The gray winter plumage of the purple sandpiper makes it one of the duller shorebirds. This bird, however, sticks out among the dunlins and sanderlings as it mingles with them, seeking food at the shoreline.

the dunlin. It can grow to 10 inches (25 cm) long. Its winter plumage includes a gray back and a white underside. It is not hard to distinguish the knot from the dunlin because resting knots gather in much denser groups. The sanderling is another bird that is similar in shape and size to the dunlin. This bird, though, is a silvery gray and has a white stripe on its wings. This stripe is very evident in flight. These three species have relatively short bills and feed mainly on invertebrates such as clam worms and macomas. They hunt their prey at depths not greater than 2 inches (4 cm). These birds have a characteristic gait, running in short steps along the line where the waves break. They follow the movement of the water, continuously scanning mud and sand in search of food.

The common sandpiper and the green sandpiper are two small species related to those previously mentioned. They have similar feeding patterns and also live in Europe. Among the American species are the spotted sandpiper and the white-rumped sandpiper. The purple sandpipers often winter together with the turnstones. They form large flocks on the most rugged areas of the estuaries and bays in west-

Bar-tailed godwits nest in the humid European and Asiatic tundras. They winter in small groups along the coasts of Great Britain, continental Europe, and northwest Africa. Like many other shorebirds, the bar-tailed godwit takes on a grayish coloration during the winter. In summer, it turns a bright red-brown.

ern Europe and northeast America. The purple sandpiper is among the few species of shorebirds that winters on the American coast north of Cape Cod. The turnstone is a bulky bird with a white back and white wings. It is appropriately named, as it is often seen turning over rocks and seaweed in search of crustaceans, mollusks and worms, which are its prey.

The purple sandpiper is slightly smaller than the turnstone but has a longer bill. Its gray-brown plumage has a purple cast. It camouflages itself among the rocks so well that it is hard to spot from a distance. It feeds on small crustaceans that it hunts along the beach.

Redshanks, Greenshanks, Curlews, Godwits, and Dowitchers

The redshank and the greenshank are European shorebirds with long legs and long bills. There are shorebirds

along the eastern coast of North America that are similar to these European birds in both appearance and choice of habitat. They are the willet, the greater yellowleg sandpiper, and the lesser yellowleg sandpiper. The redshank, well known for its bright red legs, nests in western Europe. It is called "the swamp's sentinel." Its loud warning signal, "tew-tew-tew," is heard first, before the bird is seen. Unlike the smaller shorebirds, redshanks and related varieties move slowly and gracefully along the waterline, catching small invertebrates with their pointed bills.

The largest shorebirds of the estuaries are the curlew and the godwit. Additionally, North America has the dowitcher. The bar-tailed godwit is a European species that nests in northern Scandinavia and in Russia. Its counterpart in North America is the marbled godwit. It nests inland along the United States-Canadian border. The European curlews nest all over western Europe. Curlews, godwits, and dowitchers have long bills that allow them to catch prey deep down in sand or mud. They feed on a wide selection of digging invertebrates. This includes those that bury themselves quite deep, such as some clam worms. The clam worms are caught as they back up into the rear part of their burrows to expel their droppings. It is easy to spot the godwits and curlews as they patiently wait for the worms to surface.

The Shorebirds in Their Feeding Zones

The daily movements of the shorebirds are determined by the tidal patterns.

At high tide, the feeding areas are submerged. The birds gather in flocks to rest whenever they can find a safe spot. At this time of the day, shorebirds can be observed more closely. As the tide recedes, the first birds to leave the resting areas are the smallest of the group. The ringed plover, the dunlin, and the sanderling run after the water as it recedes from the mud flats. When the mud is completely exposed, the bar-tailed godwits arrive on the scene. The curlews soon follow. The oystercatchers are the last to leave their resting area. They wait until the tide has uncovered the cockle beds in the lower shore zone.

The Surface-feeding Ducks

Large numbers of ducks, geese, and swans also dwell in the estuaries. Some of these birds are residents, others winter in the region, and still others just stop by during their

Wigeon

Teal

Wild goose

Brant

migrations. There are many varieties of ducks that spend the winter in the estuaries of western Europe and eastern America. Some are the widgeon, the teal, the mallard, the long-tailed duck, the pintail, the blackhead, and the common scoter. The velvet scoter, the black duck, and the canvasback are among the typically American species.

The shelduck is one of the few species that nest exclusively in the estuaries. It is a large bird, resembling a goose, with an extraordinary black, white, brown or dark green coloration. This species is common in western Europe. About half of its population lives on the British Isles. It nests inside burrows a short distance away from the estuary mud expanses on which it feeds. It eats mainly small snails.

The coast of western Europe is an important wintering area for many geese. In contrast, the coast of eastern America is used chiefly as a temporary rest area during the migration of these birds. In America, they winter at more southern latitudes than they do in Europe.

The smallest among the geese, and also the most dependent on the sea, is the brant. It has a circumpolar distribution and nests in the high Arctic. This bird spends the winter on the western coasts of Europe, especially in Denmark, and on the eastern coasts of North America, particularly in New Jersey. The brant usually feeds on the mud flats uncovered by the receding tide. There it finds its main diet of eelweed and green seaweed. During the winter in some areas where eelweed is scarce, these birds fly inland to graze on wheat fields. Naturally, farmers do not appreciate this.

The barnacle goose is easily recognized by its beautiful black, gray, and white plumage. The nesting area for this species is a narrow band stretching from eastern Greenland through Spitsbergen (a group of islands north of Norway) and on to northwest Russia. These birds winter on little islands off the western coast of the British Isles and Holland. Its name has a curious origin. In the Middle Ages before its nesting area was discovered, the barnacle goose was thought to develop from tree-growing barnacles, like a fruit.

The most common goose along the western coasts of the North Atlantic is the Canada goose. Numerous subspecies nest all over Canada and in the northern regions of the United States. The Canada geese that winter on the Atlantic Coast of North America reproduce mainly in Labrador, Newfoundland, and along the eastern part of Hudson Bay. This species is also established in western Europe where it

A pair of shelducks feeds in an area left uncovered at low tide. These geese eat mainly small sea snails and nest only in estuaries. Estuaries are the habitats where the shelducks can find enough food to raise litters of ten or more ducklings.

has lost most of its migratory habits. Two other European species that commonly winter in the estuaries of western Europe are the wild goose and the pink-footed goose. The wild geese spend the winter in Great Britain. In the spring, they nest in Ireland or in the northern areas of Europe. They feed mainly on farmland. In the fall, they look for barley and oat stubbles. In the winter, they find potatoes, turnips, and carrots. Most varieties of domestic geese are derived from the wild goose. The pink-footed goose, like the barnacle goose, has a very small area for reproduction. It includes Spitsbergen, eastern Greenland, and Iceland. This species winters in large flocks in only a few locations. One of these is Solway Firth, an estuary on England's northwest coast. Among the swans, the Bewick's swan nests in the Arctic and has a circumpolar distribution. It winters in the estuaries and bays that face the middle Atlantic along the coasts of North America and Western Europe.

THE MARINE BIRDS

Seabirds abound in Atlantic waters at latitudes of 40 degrees north and above on both the American and western European coasts. When it is not the nesting season, some species tend to stay closer to the coast than others. Thus, they can be grouped into coastal species, sea species, and open-sea species. During the reproductive season, all of these birds must come to land to raise their young.

The Coastal Birds

The gulls are well known not only in the North Atlantic, but all over the world as well. They not only visit harbors, beaches, and estuaries, but they also fly inland following rivers and channels. They are found in places that might seem much too far from the ocean to an observer unfamiliar with the gulls' versatility. Gulls, however, go where they must for food. Also, since they are scavengers, their diet can be varied. The gulls' pointed wings allow them to maneuver gracefully in the air. They can land effortlessly both on the ground and in the water. They have long, strong legs as well as webbed feet. They are, therefore, at ease both on land and at sea. They can walk like a raven or a pigeon does, and yet they are skilled swimmers. These birds, though, are not highly specialized. They cannot dive under the water and certainly cannot swoop onto fish from above like gannets and cormorants do. Sometimes, however, they catch fish that are swimming near the surface of water. But these are rare catches, and they are usually successful only with wounded or sick prey.

The most well-known species is the herring gull. Several varieties are found in the North Atlantic and in other areas of the Northern Hemisphere. The largest of the group is the great black-backed gull with a wingspan of up to 71 inches (180 cm). This bird preys upon the adults of many species of smaller seabirds such as puffins, guillemots, auks and storm petrels. Moreover, it often steals eggs and nestlings from the nests of seabirds even larger than itself. It is often seen standing still in groups of other gulls, waiting for the right moment to steal some morsel from them.

Three smaller species not found in Europe live in North America. They are the ring-billed gull, the laughing gull, and the Bonaparte's gull. The ring-billed gull looks like a small herring gull, but it has a very distinctive black ring on the tip of its bill. These gulls nest near fresh water all over the continent north of the Great Lakes. In winter, they move to the coasts. During the last century, these gulls also nested

Opposite: A colony of kittiwakes dots the rocky coast of southern Ireland. The rocky, jagged coasts are the home of many seabirds, mainly gulls and auks, during the nesting period. Thousands of pairs can gather on small sugarloaf promontories like the one in the picture. Each pair has a few square inches of nesting space. Sometimes the colonies are mixed, but even then the different species tend to stay separate.

Above: The common gull, a species greatly studied by ethology (study of animal behavior under natural conditions) scholars in Europe, is shown in various postures. This gull is one of the most common of its group in western Europe, both along the coast and inland. During the last century, its population has increased dramatically. This is due to its adaptation of feeding on garbage. This gull is currently also spreading along the northeastern coast of the United States.

Opposite: An unmistakable relative of the tern, the skimmer, dwells along the southeastern coast of North America. This bird has a very strange bill. Its lower part is longer than the upper part, which accounts for the bird's unusual fishing technique. As the drawing shows, these birds fly parallel to the ocean surface, "plowing" the water with the lower bill. This creates light ripples, which attract small fish and crustaceans, which are themselves looking for smaller prey. As soon as the skimmer's beak touches a fish, the upper part of the bill springs downward closing the prey in a lethal trap. Skimmers fish at dawn and at sunset when terns and gulls are resting. During the day, they rest on the shores in small groups.

in large numbers along the coast of Maine and in the Gulf of Saint Lawrence. Unfortunately, they were eagerly sought by egg and feather hunters who completely wiped out the species from the area by 1920. Today, several thousand pairs of ringed-bill gulls have come back to nest in the Gulf of Saint Lawrence, but not along the Maine coast.

The laughing gull is a warm-water species. Up until 1940, it formed large nesting colonies on small islands from off the coast of Maine all the way down to the tropics. During the last few years, though, the population of this gull has seriously decreased. This follows an increase in the number of herring gulls and lesser black-backed gulls.

Another declining species is the Bonaparte's gull. At first sight, this bird resembles the common European gull. It is smaller, though, in size and does not nest on the coast like the European gulls. Instead, it nests inland on spruce trees around lakes and swamps. This gull lives on the coast only during the winter.

There are a number of strictly European gulls that do not nest on the American Atlantic Coast. Two of these are the common gull and the lesser black-backed gull. The latter species is very similar in size and behavior to the

herring gull. Only subtle differences exist. The lesser black-backed gull has a dark gray back (the herring gull's is silver) and yellow legs (the herring gull's are pink). Moreover, there can be mixed colonies of the two species of gulls. Within these colonies, though, differences are maintained. The pairs of lesser black-backed gulls tend to prefer the flatter stretches of land, while the herring gulls choose small outcrops on sheer cliffs.

Like the herring gull, the lesser black-backed gull will venture inland looking for garbage discarded by people. When the cold season arrives, this species migrates to the Mediterranean Sea and Africa to winter. Small numbers even reach the American coast along Nova Scotia and mingle with flocks of Bonaparte's gulls.

The black skimmer is one of the most peculiar coastal birds of the Atlantic Ocean. It nests in colonies along the coasts and riverbanks of North America, but it is also found in South America. It is the only species in temperate climates belonging to the tropical family of *Rynchopidae*. The two other species of this family, very similar to the black skimmer, live in Africa and tropical Asia.

This bird, which closely resembles the tern, has short, red legs, long pointed, dark wings, a dark back, and a white underside. The skimmer's most peculiar feature, however, is a long, knifelike bill. The lower part of the bill is longer than the upper part, and in the American variety, the bill is red with a black tip.

The delicate and graceful terns are among the most beautiful of coastal birds. Also called "sea swallows," these birds are superbly adapted to a life of aerial acrobatics. They have long, pointed wings and deeply forked tails. Their legs, however, are relatively short, and not very well suited for walking or swimming.

Unlike their close relatives, the gulls, these graceful birds are by no means scavengers. On the contrary, they are first-rate fishers, able to catch their prey in a spectacular way. They soar into the air and hover almost motionless above schools of fish. They appear to carefully evaluate the situation with their bills turned downward. Suddenly they plummet, folding their wings before touching the water. They seize their prey just below the surface of the water.

Many species of terns of the North Atlantic nest along the ocean shores as well as inland by fresh water. They migrate southward when winter comes. The most well-known species are the small tern, the common tern, the sandwich tern, and the arctic tern.

An uncommon species, one whose numbers are decreasing, is the Dougall's tern. This species is very similar to the common and arctic terns. During nesting season, however, its chest takes on a delicate rosy coloration. The Dougall's tern spends the winter on the coasts of western Africa and South America. It is often caught and killed in traps baited with fish and scattered on the shore. Their choice of winter habitat has contributed to their declining numbers.

Usually terns nest in large, well-populated colonies on sandy or pebbly beaches. Many different species gather together. Reproducing in a colony increases the chances of survival of the nestlings. During the nesting period, the terns become very aggressive and attack any potential predator with determination. Even people can find themselves in trouble if they get too close to a colony. When searching for food, group nesting proves advantageous once again. Each individual in the colony keeps an eye on the good or bad luck of the others, so that the entire group soon identifies the best fishing areas. On the other hand, life in a colony also has some disadvantages. Predators, like the herring gull and

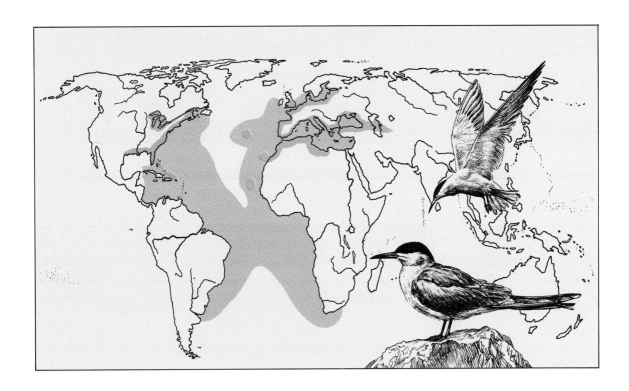

the lesser black-backed gull, are not frightened by the warnings and attacks of adult terns.

The small tern nests in sparse colonies at the high-tide line on sandy beaches often used by bathers. Its eggs are always at risk of being carried away by the waves or being trampled on by swimmers. Some people have suggested that the best way to protect this species is to locate the colonies and enclose them in wire fencing.

The Seabirds

The cormorants are typical seabirds. The various species of cormorants make up the family *Phalacrocoracidae.* Usually these are large birds, almost entirely black, with long necks and sturdy, hooked bills. They can swim under the water, easily catching the fish that form their diet. In the water, they move with their strong, webbed feet acting as flippers and their long tails acting as rudders.

Cormorants can regulate their flotation in the water. They do this by inflating numerous air sacs to various degrees, depending on their needs. The air sacs are connected to the lungs. Thanks to this feature, the cormorant is able to swim on the surface like a duck. It can also go partially under the water with only its head and neck stick-

Young crested cormorants wait in the nest. This species, like many others, nests on small ridges of sheer rock above the sea. The tufted cormorant is a strictly European species. In America, its equivalent is the double-crested cormorant. The double-crested is the most common cormorant species along the eastern Atlantic coast.

ing out. Cormorants have relatively large wings and can fly very well. They can also move under the water with ease because their feathers are not waterproof. This means that under the water these birds become soaking wet. No air bubbles are trapped in their feathers to hinder diving. However, there is a price to pay for this ability to move so freely under the water. In order to fly effectively, when these birds emerge from the water, they have to spend a long time waiting for their feathers to dry. They spread their wings wide open in a very distinctive posture.

Among the various species found on the Atlantic coast, the common cormorant is widespread both in America and in Europe. In America, it does not venture farther south than Maine. In Europe and Asia, on the other hand, it is very common along inland lakes and seas all the way to China, Japan, and southern Russia.

Some species of cormorants develop a tuft of feathers on their heads during the mating season. The double-crested cormorant, a North American species, has two tufts, one on each side of its head. This species nests all along the

Two black auks display their summer plumage. The dark, even coloration is useful for camouflaging the birds ashore as they brood their eggs. In winter, the black auks have white bellies, like all other auks. This coloration is also good camouflage. Seen from above, their dark backs blend in with the color of the ocean. Seen from below, their white undersides are almost invisible in the reflections off the water's surface.

eastern and western coasts of Canada and the United States. It is an almost perfect ecological counterpart to the European shag cormorant.

Crested cormorants, both the American and European species, closely resemble the common cormorant but are a little smaller. They have an even coloration with green tints and one or two tufts of feathers on their heads.

Unlike the common cormorants that live on both inland waters and along the coasts, the crested cormorants are found only along the coastlines. There they manage to avoid direct food competition with the common cormorants by exhibiting quite distinct food preferences. Crested cormorants feed in open waters, mainly catching sand lan-

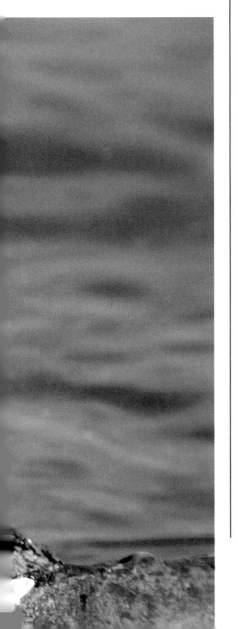

ces, herrings, sardines, and shads. The common cormorants, on the other hand, fish near the coast. Their main diet includes shrimp and flatfish like sole and turbot.

The auk family is another group of seabirds. The birds of the auk family are even more specialized fishers than the cormorants, but they are relatively poor flyers. Their wings, in fact, have became very small as part of their extreme adaptation to underwater swimming.

These birds remain in open waters all of the time and come to shore only to nest. In the Northern Hemisphere they occupy the same ecological niche as the penguins do in the Southern Hemisphere. Six species are found in the Atlantic Ocean. They are the little auk, the razorbill, the foolish guillemot, the Brünnich's guillemot, the black guillemot, and the puffin.

The razorbill and the Brünnich's guillemot are essentially arctic species. The other four species are well known to the bird-watchers who visit the coasts of Great Britain, Denmark, and northern France. Razorbills and foolish guillemots lay their eggs on narrow outcrops or ledges on rocky walls. They do not build an actual nest. The eggs of these birds are shaped like pears, so that if pushed, they tend to move in a circle and do not roll off the ledge.

Razorbills tend to nest inside natural hollows in rocks. Foolish guillemots nest close to each other on sheer, narrow ridges above the sea. Apparently, these birds need social stimuli, such as the other birds' noise and activity, in order to nest successfully. Even when there is a lot of space, they tend to gather in a small area to reproduce.

The most colorful and attractive seabirds of the North Atlantic are the puffins. These birds have large, triangular bills with red, yellow, and blue stripes. A large part of the entire Atlantic population, which is between eight and ten million pairs, nests in Ireland. Another significant number will choose the Westman Islands off the southern Icelandic coast as their nesting site. The remainder of the European population is scattered mainly along the coasts of Norway, the British Isles, and the Faeroe Islands. The American population nests mainly on little islands in Witless Bay (Newfoundland).

The puffin's nest is dug in the ground. It may be either freshly dug, or it may be a remodeled rabbit burrow. In time, the continuous digging produces a lot of loose ground. Eventually the entire site will be useless for new nests. At this point, the colony may gradually diminish. The last

At the end of its reproduction season, the puffin loses the colorful, horny covering of its bill piece by piece. The bill was an important feature during courtship. Also, their pure white cheeks turn gray and look more like their dark backs. Puffins will regain their bright bill coloration in the spring. The bill is used as a tool to dig nest tunnels as deep as 16 feet (5 m).

Summer

Parts of the bill are lost at the end of the reproduction season.

Winter

remaining pairs will be forced to move elsewhere. The puffin, small and relatively helpless, needs to build its nest in a tunnel to protect itself and the nestlings from predators. The puffin's predators include gulls and jaegers, which are large, strong-flying birds that tend to harass weaker ones.

The puffin's peculiar bill is very useful for carrying many small fish at one time. Puffins also like small herring. One of the reasons for the decrease in the puffin population might be that the numbers of its favorite prey, the herring, are also decreasing. To combat both decreases, less valuable species of fish than the herring have been used to prepare fishmeal and fertilizers in recent years.

The puffins themselves are traditionally preyed upon by humans in some areas of the North Atlantic. Sometimes they are caught with nets or in their burrows during the nesting season. Today, they are hunted mostly in July at the end of the nesting season. A device called a "fleygastong" is used. This is, essentially, a huge, triangular "butterfly net," fixed at the end of a long pole. It is used mainly on the Faeroe Islands. The birds are lured toward the rim of a rocky wall, often by the use of mounted puffins as decoys. Once there, they are trapped in the nets that the hunters skillfully maneuver in the air.

This kind of hunt is limited today to a few areas along the North Atlantic coast. Usually these areas do not have any major economic resources. The practice is strictly controlled to limit the damage to the bird populations. Unfortunately, in the past, things were different. Many seabird populations were heavily exploited. The worst case was that of the great auk, which is now extinct due to excessive hunting. It was a large, black-and-white bird, closely related to the razorbill. It was 30 inches (75 cm) tall and completely incapable of flying. At first sight, it resembled a large penguin. It was a clumsy and vulnerable land animal. In the water, however, it was swift, supple, and almost impossible to catch. Its area of distribution covered both sides of the North Atlantic, but it did not live at the northernmost polar latitudes.

Every year, just like the auks still living today, the great auk would land to lay its pear-shaped egg on small islands off the coast of northern Europe, Iceland, and Newfoundland. Both the adults and the eggs have been hunted for a very long time. This, in fact, played a central role in the colonization of North America. They were an excellent source of food and oil for the first explorers and fishermen.

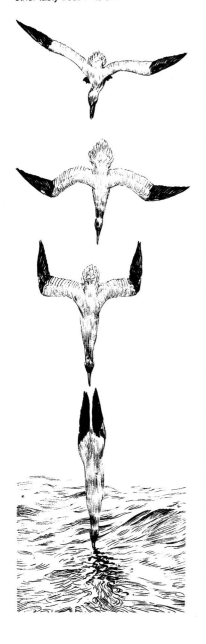

When fishing, the solan goose dives down from a height of over 82 feet (25 m) and sometimes enters the water at a speed of over 62 miles (100 km) per hour. At the moment of impact, its shape is highly hydrodynamic (efficient at moving through water) like that of a missile or a torpedo. It can take advantage of the speed and dive down 39 to 49 feet (12 to 15 m). It uses its wings and feet to swim. This bird can stay under the water for over ten seconds and will eventually emerge with a herring, a mackerel, or some other tasty treat in its bill.

At first, hunting was relatively limited, and the great auks withstood the impact. At the beginning of the eighteenth century, things changed. Intense commercial exploitation aimed primarily at auk feathers rather than meat began. Hunters would raid colonies and club the adults to death. They would boil them in order to pluck their feathers. Showing even greater disregard for the value of the birds, they often would burn them whole in order to keep the fire under the boiling pots going. By 1830, the entire population of great auks had been wiped out with the exception of one colony. This last colony was on Geirfuglasker Island, a remote spot off the coast of Iceland. Unfortunately, in 1830 most members of this last group were killed by a volcanic eruption. The few surviving auks found shelter on Eldey Island, where they were again persecuted by hunters of feathers and eggs. Finally, in 1844, several sailors landed on the island and found only two remaining individuals and one egg. For reasons known only to themselves, they broke open the egg and killed the pair. Since then, no individuals of this species have been seen.

One of the largest and most spectacular Atlantic seabirds is the solan goose. It could have been the subject of the same type of ill-fated story as the great auk. The adults of this species are as much as 36 inches (92 cm) long, with a wingspan of 67 to 71 inches (170 to 180 cm). They are white, with black wing tips and a light yellow neck. The entire world population of solan geese nests in twenty-two colonies in the North Atlantic.

People have always exploited the solan geese, hunting them for their eggs, meat, and feathers. The nestlings, called "gugas," are tender and fat and are considered a real delicacy. One of the largest colonies in the world was at Bird Rock in the Gulf of Saint Lawrence. In the early nineteenth century, it was the home of 125,000 nesting pairs. These birds were hunted so extensively that in 1900 only a few pairs remained. In the last century, the solan goose has been more carefully protected. Its populations are presently undergoing a strong increase at a rate of about 3 percent a year.

The solan geese spend about eight months a year in very crowded colonies on the ridges of sheer cliffs above the sea or on small rocky islands. In winter, they migrate south and can often be seen in the Mediterranean Sea area. Their nests are built with seaweed glued together by their droppings. They are spaced with extreme care such that each

During the winter months, solan geese are common all over the northern Atlantic. When they reproduce, however, they concentrate in a few colonies, each numbering thousands of nesting pairs. It is surprising that each individual is able to find its nest in the incredible chaos of these huge gatherings. The parents seem to know every aspect of how the colony works. They are able to recognize their single offspring by voice.

brooding bird is just out of the pecking range of its closest neighbor. When brooding, many birds develop an "incubation plate" on their undersides. This plate is a bare patch of skin densely laced with blood vessels. It supplies much heat to the egg. The solan goose, however, develops an incubation plate on its webbed feet. It broods its egg by enfolding it in its feet.

The young solan geese take on a dark gray plumage

following the loss of their white "nest" down. The plumage turns white again, gradually, in a sequence of yearly molts throughout the first four to five years. During this period, the birds are still not fully mature and do not build nests. In many cases, the young do not even go back to the nesting areas, but instead stay in the southern seas the whole year round. The European populations are off the coasts of Africa and southern Europe. The American populations stay around the Gulf of Mexico.

The Open-sea Birds

Shearwaters, fulmars, and storm petrels all belong to the order Procellariiformes. They are all adapted to living almost permanently in the open sea. Their nostrils are very unusual. They are modified into horny, little tubes that are attached to the top part of the bill.

The various species of birds are specialized for feeding on different types of food. The largest of the family, the fulmars, are mostly scavengers and collect the remains of fish and other material off the water's surface. The shearwater is smaller than the fulmar. It preys on small fish, squid, and crustaceans that it finds on the surface of the water or just beneath. The tiny storm petrels eat mostly zooplankton. These small crustaceans collect on the water's surface. Since these organisms are often present in large numbers, the storm petrels' numbers can also be very high.

These open-sea birds are highly successful in their environment. This is due largely to their exceptional flying skills. They are able to use to perfection the air currents associated with waves. Some zoologists think that their tube-nostrils might contribute to their flying precision. They sense air pressure changes and, therefore, actually measure wind speed. A special set of glands, the "salt glands," are connected to the nostrils. These glands eliminate excess salt from the seawater that the birds drink (they never drink fresh water). These birds also have a much more acute sense of smell than many other birds.

Shearwaters and storm petrels nest in structures resembling puffin tunnels. They do this in order to avoid attacks from predators, especially gulls. When these birds land, they are particularly clumsy and helpless. They fly in and out of their nests only at night. It is likely that these birds use their acute sense of smell to find their tunnels and their partners. The birds themselves give off a strong, moldy scent.

When threatened or frightened, both shearwaters and

The fulmar is a typical open-sea bird, even though it looks like a gull. Gulls live almost exclusively near the coast. This bird has the tube-nostrils typical of the order *Procelariiformes* (comprising fulmars, petrels, and shearwaters). Like all other birds of this group, it catches its food in the open sea. When their only egg hatches, the adults feed the young with concentrated stomach oil. Carrying food from the fishing areas would be extremely tiring and impractical.

fulmars can regurgitate an oil from their stomachs. It has an especially unpleasant smell. The nestlings of the fulmars are particularly well known for their habit of spitting this oil through their bills and nostrils. They can accurately aim at any intruders who come too close to their nest.

When it is not nesting season, the birds of this species scatter over the huge expanses of ocean. They gather mainly around fishing areas where the fishermen throw the leftovers from fish processing overboard.

The fulmars live for a long time and have relatively low reproduction rates. Like the solan geese, they do not achieve sexual maturity before five years of age. They raise only one offspring during each reproductive season. In spite of this, during the last century their numbers have been rapidly increasing. They have been pushing their way farther and farther south. In 1878, only a small colony of twelve pairs was living on the British Isles, having just settled in Shetland (the northernmost county of Scotland). Today, approximately 300,000 pairs nest on any suitable spot on the narrow ridges of the sheer cliffs above the sea.

Among the species of shearwaters, one of the most

The fork-tailed petrel is another ocean species that chooses small islands in the open sea for its reproduction. The islands are usually made up of rocks and peat-moors. In fact, these birds dig their nests in the peat, sometimes under a rock. Like all ocean species, these petrels lay a single egg each year. They rear their young for seven weeks. The incubation and rearing period for sea birds depends upon how far they have to go to catch their food. Birds of the open sea have rather long maturation periods.

famous is the manx shearwater. This species nests on many small islands around Great Britain and Ireland and in the Mediterranean Sea. It does not reach North America. The shearwaters' legs are attached toward the back of its body. This makes these birds excellent swimmers but very poor walkers. They are slow and clumsy on land. This makes them especially vulnerable to predators when they come ashore. Some great black-backed gulls actually specialize in preying on shearwaters. The gulls kill them with just a few pecks on the head. It is no wonder that the shearwaters are so reluctant to come ashore. Sometimes they must come to shore when they are tending their young or brooding. Toward sundown they gather by the hundreds close to the coast on the ocean surface. They stay together, floating like rafts, and wait for darkness to come before they dare venture onto land.

The smallest birds of the group, the storm petrels, can sometimes be seen as they soar in their unique way. They move about somewhat like a moth does, with their legs dangling down almost touching the water's surface. Perhaps this habit explains their name. Petrels, just like their namesake Saint Peter, seem to be able to walk on water.

The kittiwake is the only species of the gull group that has adapted to life at sea. Consequently, its nesting habits and its behavior patterns have also changed. Its social life is strictly bound to the cliffs. This picture was taken on the Farne Islands, a group of sixteen very small islands off the northeastern coast of England's Northumberland County.

60

The fulmar is the largest bird of the order *Procellariformes* living in the North Atlantic. One of the peculiar features of these birds is the tube-nostrils. These grow on top of the bill, which is composed of numerous horny plates.

The North Atlantic has two nesting species of open-sea birds. The common storm petrel has its population, like that of the manx shearwater, divided into many colonies. They live on the European side of the North Atlantic coast as well as in the Mediterranean Sea area. The fork-tailed petrel, on the other hand, nests only along the Atlantic coast, in both Europe and America.

A third species found in the Atlantic Ocean, often in large numbers, is the Wilson's petrel. It nests in the Antarctic Ocean, off the southeastern coast of South America. It migrates north during the winter season in the Southern Hemisphere.

The Wilson's petrel is very similar to the common storm petrel. The only difference is the bright yellow coloring of the Wilson's petrel's legs. It is probably the most abundant seabird species in the world.

The open-sea birds just described have an interesting companion in their remote marine environment. This bird is the kittiwake. A member of the gull group, the kittiwake, shares the same habitat and some of the same behavior patterns with them.

The kittiwake is smaller than the herring gull but resembles it in adult plumage. Its back is light gray and the rest of its body is white. This bird also has a yellow bill and black legs and wing tips. It is missing the white spots found on other gull species. The young kittiwake has a black bill, a black band on the forehead, and another black band diagonally across the wings. The real peculiarity of the kittiwake is not its appearance, which is quite similar to that of other members of its family. This bird is unique because, unlike other gulls, it is a true open-sea dweller. It skillfully fishes both on the surface and some inches below it. Like all gulls, though, it likes scraps of fish. Kittiwakes often gather in large numbers in the commercial fishing areas of the north.

The kittiwakes nest in large colonies on sheer rocky coasts across almost all of the Northern Hemisphere. They are often seen together with auks and puffins. They build cup-shaped nests with seaweed on tiny ridges in the rocks. Here they raise their young. The major threat to nestlings is falling off the cliffs. In order to avoid this, the young remain still most of the time. They turn their backs to the precipice even when the parents arrive with a beak full of food. Moreover, the young seem particularly cautious when venturing out of the nest. Although they can fly at thirty-five days, they do not usually leave the nest as soon as that.

FISH AND COMMERCIAL FISHING

Some of the best fishing areas in the world are located in the North Atlantic. They include Georges Bank off Cape Cod, the Grand Bank southeast of Newfoundland, the banks around the Faeroe Islands and Iceland, and Dogger Bank in the North Sea, between England and continental Europe. Not very long ago, these banks were dry land, emerging only slightly from the ocean. Even today, fishermen who work in these areas often pull remains of prehistoric trees or animals to the surface.

The waters of the banks and of the continental shelf where the banks are located are shallow. Therefore, basic nutrients, especially phosphates and nitrates, are easily brought up from the bottom by the stirring action of the wind and the currents. As on land, these nutrients plus sunlight, carbon dioxide, and water are the essential ingredients for plant life. These essential ingredients form the basis for the principal food chains.

Phytoplankton and Fish

Plant life in the oceans is represented by phytoplankton. It is formed by huge quantities of microscopic algae adrift in the water. The phytoplankton carries on photosynthesis (the transforming of carbon dioxide and water into complex sugars by using sunlight). Phytoplankton grows and multiplies only if sunlight filters through the water. In the North Atlantic, light can reach down to 98 feet (30 m). The nutrients are most easily renewed in winter when the winds are strongest. But the phytoplankton cannot start rapid growth until spring, when the water temperature rises. After very rapid spring growth, a period follows during which the basic nutrients have been exhausted.

A second peak in the quantity of phytoplankton occurs during the fall storms before the cold winter temperatures take over. It is due to the turnover of water from the bottom to the surface. In some areas, this turnover may be a constant occurrence. This is true in the Grand Bank where the warm Gulf Stream meets the cold Labrador Current. Here nutrients are quickly recycled. Phytoplankton productivity is high for most of the year, except in winter. As a consequence, the Grand Bank is exceptionally rich in quantities of cod and other fish that feed off the phytoplankton. The area has attracted fishermen for centuries.

Another area just as teeming with fish is located in the North Sea, between Great Britain and continental Europe. Water movements are only partially responsible for the

Opposite: Cod are hung to dry in the sun on the Lofoten Islands off Norway's northwestern coast. The waters of the northern seas are among the richest fishing grounds in the world. They are also among the most heavily exploited by people.

The distribution of plankton in the North Atlantic is the main factor determining the distribution of the schools of fish. The values on the map refer to the concentration of plankton biomass (the mass of all living plankton components).

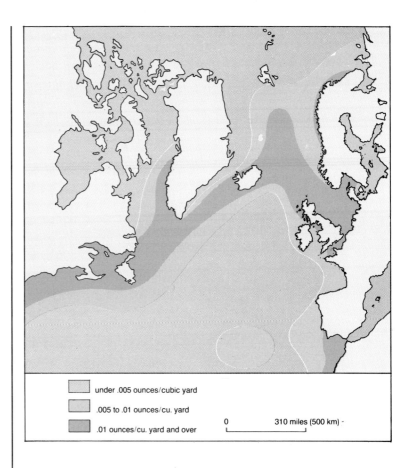

under .005 ounces/cubic yard

.005 to .01 ounces/cu. yard

.01 ounces/cu. yard and over

0   310 miles (500 km)

fertility of this region. Some major north European rivers, such as the Rhine, the Elbe, and the Weser, flow into the ocean at this point. This keeps the ocean waters replenished with nutrients. Another explanation for the abundance of fish is that the waters of the North Sea are always being stirred up. This is due to the merging of two branches of the Gulf Stream that flow along the north and south sides of the British Isles.

Ocean fish are often grouped according to the depths at which they live. Those dwelling close to the surface are called pelagic, or open-sea fish. The ones living close to or on the bottom are called bottom fish. Some bottom fish such as flounder and plaice, which is a type of flatfish, prefer shallow bottom waters. Others, like cod and its relative, the hake, live at depths of several hundred feet.

The Food Chains

Most phytoplankton is formed from two groups of unicellular plants, the diatoms and the dinoflagellates. The diatoms are the most abundant and are often attached in long chains. Their siliceous shell (made of silica compounds) is ornamented with spikes and ridges. This helps them stay afloat in the surface-water layer where sunlight can reach them. The dinoflagellates also try to stay in the area lit by the sun. Unlike the diatoms, they can move about. Each cell of this plant is equipped with two whip-like appendages called "flagella." One is used for horizontal movements. The other is enclosed in a crease on its shell and is used for rotating movements. Some dinoflagellates give off light, especially when jostled. On dark nights, their presence is revealed by a dim glow on the ocean's surface. Phytoplankton is eaten by many animals, most of which are part of the zooplankton. Zooplankton is made up of the animal members of the plankton community. Phytoplankton-eaters are of varying sizes. They range from unicellular protozoans with elaborate shells to the largest jellyfish, which can be 6 feet (2 m) in diameter. Depending upon the time of the year, zooplankton can contain fish eggs and larvae, crustaceans, or mollusks. There are medium-sized organisms that remain zooplankton throughout their lives. These include various types of worms and other invertebrates. The most important are the copepods (tiny crustaceans) and a group of crustaceans belonging to the order

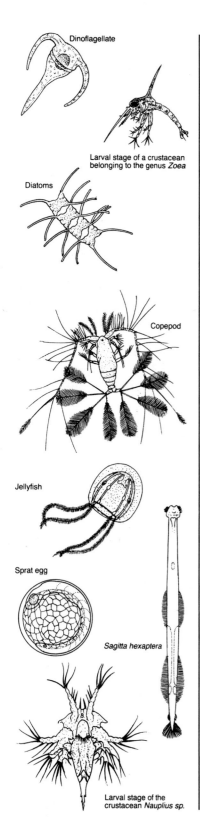

Dinoflagellate

Larval stage of a crustacean belonging to the genus *Zoea*

Diatoms

Copepod

Jellyfish

Sprat egg

Sagitta hexaptera

Larval stage of the crustacean *Nauplius sp.*

Euphasiacea. To avoid predators, the copepods migrate into deeper waters during the day and come back to the surface at night. In this way, they feed under the protection of darkness.

Plankton, in general, is defined as forms of plant or animal life that float in the sea, as distinguished from coastal or bottom forms. It is eaten by open-sea fish, squid, seabirds, and many sedentary, filtering animals such as clams, mussels, and barnacles. Herring mainly feed on copepods. Other fish prefer phytoplankton. Usually these fish filter the water, trapping the phytoplankton with their specially-modified gills. The huge basking shark has also adapted to feed on filtered plankton. This particular shark may grow up to 39 feet (12 m) in length and weigh over four tons. Small open-sea fish can be prey to bottom fish as well as to larger pelagic fish such as salmon, mackerel, and tuna.

When marine plants and animals die, they fall to the ocean floor. They become food for small filtering invertebrates and debris-eaters. These debris-eaters, which include many sea worms, get their food in an interesting way. They ingest the substrate (the base on which an organism lives), digest any part that is edible, and expel the rest. These small animals are preyed upon by larger worms, shrimp, mollusks, crustaceans, and starfish. All of these predators, together with their prey, are a rich source of food for bottom fish such as flounder and plaice. Other fish, like cod, haddock, saddled bream (sunfish), and small sharks have a mixed diet of open-sea fish and invertebrates.

Open-water Fish

The most well-known open-sea fish of the Atlantic Ocean belong to the herring family. Besides the herring, this group also includes sardine, sprat (European herring), menhaden, and shad.

Herring are very common. They are found off both the eastern and western coasts of the North Atlantic and are represented by many different species. These fish reproduce in cold coastal waters. Each female can produce twenty to fifty thousand eggs that, unlike those of other fish, do not float. Instead they fall to the sea floor where they stick to seaweed and rocks. Herring spawning time coincides with periods of rapid plankton growth. The result is that the newborn larvae find plenty of food.

By the end of their first year, the young fish measure about 3 inches (7 to 8 cm) in length. They remain close to the

Opposite: Some organisms of phytoplankton and zooplankton are pictured. These plant and animal life-forms are the basis of food chains in the ocean. Some animals are part of the plankton group only at certain stages in their lives. These include starfish, sea urchins, and bivalves. These animals are free swimmers in their larval stage, but become more or less tied to the sea floor in adulthood. The same is true for the eggs of many fish, such as the sprat.

Above: The Atlantic salmon *Salmo salar.* The timing of salmon journeys changes from river to river. It can also change during the course of the years. Whenever it occurs, these animals stop eating as they start their journey. They will not eat again until spawning time, which is usually not before fall.

coast for three to seven years until they have reached a length of 10 inches (25 cm). Then they move into deeper waters. They join the adults in their feeding or wintering areas, returning to the coastal waters only to spawn.

After the herring, the mackerel is probably the most important ocean fish commercially harvested in the North Atlantic. This fish has an eye-catching iridescent pattern of dark, zigzag stripes on its back and a silvery white underside. In spring and summer, the mackerel behaves like a true open-sea fish. It forms small, compact schools and often mingles with herring. During this period, its diet consists mainly of zooplankton. It also reproduces, releasing numerous floating eggs in the water. After spawning, the adults move away from deep waters and change their diets to feed on small fish. Their main prey are young herring, sprats, and sand lances. In the fall, they leave the surface waters. They spend the winter, without eating anything, on the sea floor. They return to the surface in spring to feed on zooplankton and, eventually, go back to the areas where they were born.

Another ocean fish of the North Atlantic, often not considered a true sea fish, is the Atlantic salmon. These fish do spend most of their adult lives in the ocean. During their ocean phase, salmon visit the coasts of Greenland and Norway to feed on herring, sprats, and sand lances. They migrate from the ocean into fresh waters to spawn. For this reason, they are called "anadromous" fish. For almost a year, they swim up rivers and streams, entering them both from the eastern and western coasts of the North Atlantic.

Newborn salmon remain in fresh water for one to five years. They feed on insect larvae and small worms. Then they swim back to the ocean. During their freshwater stage, young salmon, called "parr," learn to recognize the smell of the streams where they were born. This knowledge will be important when, as adults, these fish must come back to their spawning areas. They will use their sense of smell to guide them.

The larval form of the eel, called the "leptocephalus," usually drifts in the Gulf Stream. The eel's reproduction cycle is the exact opposite of the salmon's. Instead of migrating to fresh waters to reproduce, eels spawn in the ocean. They stay there throughout their larval stage and move to fresh water when they approach adulthood. Fish with this kind of reproductive cycle are called "catadromous."

Anadromous fish are typical of northern waters. Conversely, catadromous fish are found in tropical waters. The common eel, for example, reproduces in the warm waters of the Sargasso Sea. The sea, which is part of the North Atlantic, extends from the West Indies to the Azores. There are at least two species of eels. The first is the American eel, which reproduces in the Sargasso Sea at the beginning of spring and in summer. The second is the European eel, which spawns at the same time, but more to the north.

Bottom Fish

The most important bottom fish is the cod. It belongs to the same family as the hake, the haddock, and the whiting. This fish has a bulky body and a square tail. Its variable coloration depends upon its environment. It is gray on sandy bottoms and brown or reddish in seaweed stretches. It can be almost 5 feet (1.5 m) long and weigh over 88 pounds (40 kg). The ones usually caught average 24 pounds (11 kg).

Different varieties of cod, similar to herring species, have different migration and reproduction patterns. The European cod tends to migrate more than the North American cod. For example, the Icelandic cod reproduces on the southwestern coast of Ireland but returns to its feeding areas in northern Greenland every year.

Opposite: Shown are some of the most important commercial fish found in the North Atlantic Ocean. The quantity of valuable fish in these waters is drastically decreasing due to overfishing. For this reason, the fishing industry is turning to the use of new resources.

From top to bottom, from left to right: mackerel, herring, *Brevoortia tirannus,* tuna, salmon (open-sea fish); whiting, haddock, cod, flounder, and European flounder.

The cod is only one of the 150 species of the *Gadidae* family. Almost all are found in the North Atlantic and almost all to some degree are commercially harvested. The members of this group are neritic, which means they inhabit the water near the seacoast. They come very close to the shallow coast only during spawning periods. Afterwards, they return to deeper waters. At reproduction time, all the members of this family show complex territorial behaviors.

The spawning period usually extends from February to June. Females lay up to fifteen million eggs that float until hatching time two weeks later. Such a large quantity of eggs assures the survival of a fair number of individuals. The large numbers are necessary because cod is heavily preyed upon by herring and other open-sea fish. At three to four months of age, young cod move to the ocean bottom. For some years, they migrate up and down, depending on the seasons. In summer, they dwell in surface waters, while in winter, they move into deeper waters. Finally, one year before achieving maturity, they join adult schools. There they learn the entire migratory route between the feeding areas and reproduction areas.

The strangest among the bottom fish are the flatfish. These species are very well adapted to the ocean floor, where they lie on their right or left side. The two sides of their bodies grow at different rates. At some point a flatfish's skull twists to one side or the other and its head rests on the bottom. The eye facing down shifts more or less to the top of the head. Thus, both eyes are functioning. This process of change, called a "metamorphosis," begins only after the fish has reached a certain length and has started to live on the

The European flounder is one of the many flatfish belonging to the order *Pleuronectiformes*. During their larval stage, these fish have symmetrical bodies. They undergo a metamorphosis when they start their bottom-dwelling life. The lower eye moves onto the upper side of the fish's head. At the same time, the fish takes on camouflage coloration. Usually, turbot lie down on their left sides, while flounder lie on their right sides.

sea bottom. In fact, the newborn flatfish closely resemble most other fish. They are symmetrical and swim in a natural upright position at first.

The most common flatfish is the flounder. It roams the ocean floor of the North Atlantic at depths between 984 and 3,281 feet (300 to 1,000 m). Here the temperature is between 41 and 45 degrees Fahrenheit (5 to 7 degrees Celsius). These fish are very aggressive predators. They wait for their prey by remaining motionless on the bottom. They are perfectly camouflaged with the background and ready to pounce on their victims. Their prey includes other flatfish, cod, sand lances, cephalopods such as squid and octopus, and crustaceans. Flounder grow to over 7 feet (2.4 m) long and weigh over 700 pounds (318 kg).

Exploitation by People

Traditionally, the most commercially important fish in the North Atlantic are herring and cod. In the twelfth century, herring fishing was the main industry in the Baltic Sea. Its development began with the Hanseatic League of northern Germany. The Hanseatic League was a medieval con-

On the left is a net used to catch neritic fish, like the cod, and flatfish. The net is shaped like a large funnel and is dragged along the sea floor. It is opened vertically by small buoys attached to its rim. It is kept open by two large boards, which remain apart due to the water. In the three center illustrations, pelagic fish (herring and others) are caught with a net that changes shape. The net is lowered around the school of fish and its base, still open, is drawn to the bottom by weights. A series of buoys marks its position on the surface. When the net is spread completely open, its base is narrowed and closed with a rope. When the net has taken on the shape of a bag, it is lifted on board with its load of fish. On the right, a long line is used in place of dragging nets when the ocean floor is too rough. Numerous secondary lines are attached to the main line, each one with baited hooks. At the end of the main line there is an anchor. Its position is marked by a buoy.

federation of German cities, which formed in the 1200s for trading purposes. Sometime between 1416 and 1425, the herring disappeared. This was probably due to a change in the ocean currents. It caused the ruin of the herring industry in these towns. More or less during the same period, another center for the herring industry developed in Holland. It utilized fishing areas in the North Sea. New methods of herring processing were discovered. The British herring industry did not develop until the eighteenth century. It was aided by government grants of money. Today, even though the quantity of fish has sharply decreased, all the coastal nations of northern Europe specialize in herring fishing. Norway and Russia, in particular, play a major role.

Since early times, the cod and a close relative, the haddock, have formed the basis of the fishing industry on the western coast of Europe. These fish have less fat than herring, so they are easily preserved by either drying or salting. They are a very important commercial product.

Since the twelfth century, cod has been fished in deep waters by the Basques. These people, inhabitants of the western Pyrenes mountains on the Bay of Biscay, were true pioneers in this business. Beginning with the fifteenth century, expeditions were organized from bases located in the southern part of the North Sea. They searched for cod off the coasts of northern Norway and around Iceland.

In 1497, John Cabot discovered the island of New-foundland. Its waters teemed with fish. This immediately

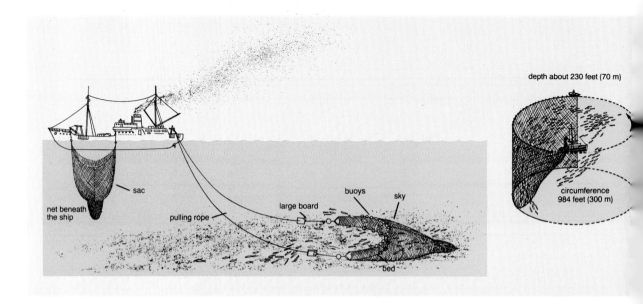

depth about 230 feet (70 m)

sac

net beneath the ship

pulling rope

large board

buoys

sky

circumference 984 feet (300 m)

bed

aroused the interest of all the north European countries involved in fishing. In particular, from the sixteenth century on, the French, Portuguese, and Germans greatly increased their fishing in the Grand Bank area. In the eighteenth century, cod fishing also developed on the American continent off New England, where several English colonies had already been established.

Around the end of the nineteenth century, herring fishing rapidly grew in America. Around this period, fishermen on both sides of the Atlantic Ocean began to realize that fish were not an endless resource. It became necessary to regulate the growth of the fishing industry. It had been expanding by leaps and bounds due to the use of more efficient technology. In this same century, sailboats were replaced by the much more powerful steamboats. This increased the catch from dragging nets across the water.

The problem of fish conservation began to be scientifically studied in the early 1900s. In 1902, the International Council for Sea Exploration was founded in Copenhagen. Every year, this institution coordinates scientific information on the location and quantity of schools of fish in the northeast Atlantic. Similar studies are performed by other institutions for the northwest Atlantic. They determine the fish species and the amount of catch that the members of the council are permitted to harvest. Moreover, other regulations determine the minimum mesh size of the fishing nets. This prevents the catching of fish under a certain size.

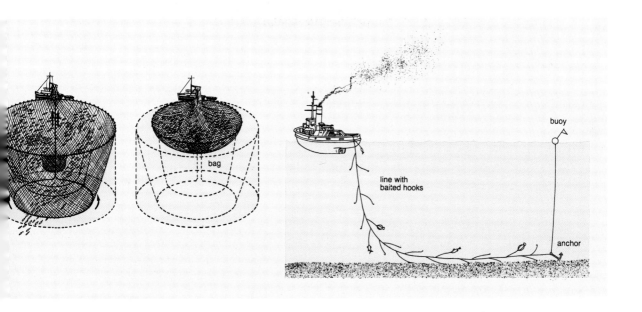

73

THE SEA MAMMALS

Two groups of sea mammals are found in the North Atlantic. They are the pinnipeds and the cetaceans. Pinnipeds, which include seals and walruses, are carnivorous aquatic mammals with all four limbs modified into flippers. Cetaceans, which include whales, dolphins, and porpoises, are also aquatic mammals. They have large heads, fishlike bodies, and paddle-shaped forelimbs. These two groups are quite different from each other. They both originated independently about fifty million years ago from terrestrial mammals, usually having four legs. Just like every other mammal, these animals can completely regulate their body temperature, so they are also called "warm-blooded animals." They also breathe air from the atmosphere. For this reason, they have developed special adaptations in order to live in the ocean.

Physiological and Anatomical Adaptations

The bodies of pinnipeds and cetaceans are tapered to move in the water with the minimum possible friction. Their limbs are modified into paddle-shaped fins or steering tails in the rear. Seals can stay under the water from five to forty minutes, depending on the species. They plunge to depths of 1,148 feet (350 m) or more. The largest whales, in turn, can dive down to 3,281 feet (1,000 m) and remain there for up to one hour.

Unlike human divers, both pinnipeds and cetaceans have special physical adaptations to avoid decompression problems. When a scuba diver plunges into the water, the nitrogen contained in the lungs tends to dissolve in the bloodstream. This is due to the increased pressure at greater depths. The deeper the diver goes, the more nitrogen that will pass into the blood. When the diver comes back to the surface, the pressure decreases. The gas dissolved in the blood is gradually released. If the dive has been deeper than about 46 feet (14 m) and if the ascent is too rapid, the nitrogen will be released too quickly. In this case, it can form gas bubbles which tend to clog blood vessels leading to vital organs. The result, called the "bends," causes serious pain and, in the worst cases, even death.

Seals avoid this problem by completely emptying their lungs before a dive. They store their oxygen in another way. Their bodies chemically bind the oxygen with special binding pigments. These are hemoglobin in the blood and myoglobin in the muscles.

The cetaceans also store oxygen in this "bound" form.

Opposite: The elegant swimming of white-sided dolphins can often be admired from a ship.

Unlike the pinnipeds, they do not empty their lungs before a dive. On the contrary, they fill them with air before diving. They deal with decompression problems in another way. They compress their lungs to the smallest possible volume using their ribs (which are not attached to the chest bone as in land mammals). The air which fills the lungs is transferred to the windpipes and air sacs. Unlike the lungs, these are densely laced with a net of capillary blood vessels. Any nitrogen that might be released from the blood during a rise to the surface would be absorbed by a fatty substance formed inside the lungs. This substance, together with water vapor, is the main component of the well-known "blow" that the cetaceans give off as they surface.

Both pinnipeds and cetaceans have developed still other devices to save oxygen. During a dive, their heartbeats markedly decrease. It drops from sixty beats a minute to thirty in the killer whale and from eighty to ten in most seals. Moreover, the entire circulatory system is modified. The

brain receives a constant blood flow throughout the time beneath the water. Blood flow to the skin, muscles, and the digestive system is sharply reduced.

The thick fat layer called "blubber," which accumulates under the skin of both groups, also has important functions. First, it helps to keep body temperature constant. Second, it is a source of energy, ready to use if food is scarce. This is especially important for whales that winter in the southern seas where there is not much for them to eat. The organisms they feed upon, small crustaceans called "krill," are practically non-existent outside of cold waters. Finally, because fat is lighter than water, it helps animals to float. A fat animal will stay on the surface with less effort and thus burn less energy than a lean animal.

The Seals

The North Atlantic has no sea lions or walruses. Only seals, belonging to the Phocidae family, dwell in these waters. These animals have short, furry, front legs and well-developed hind legs. The hind legs are modified into a type of tail, which can be compared to a cetacean's tail. Seals use their "tails" to move in the water. Powerful up and down strokes are followed by a winding movement of the entire rear part of their bodies. When on land, seals keep their rear fins lifted and move by crawling on their undersides. They arch and stretch their bellies alternately, the way a worm or a legless larva would in order to move.

Seals feed on fish—many of which are commercially important fish—invertebrates, and sometimes small seabirds. When hunting, they count on their very acute senses of hearing and vision. These work perfectly even under water. Moreover, at shorter distances, the seal can use its refined sense of touch. The bristles of its whiskers and "eyebrows" serve as receptors for this sense.

Seals are gregarious animals and are often seen resting in large groups on land, on sandbanks, or along rocky coasts. They bask in the sun (sometimes in positions closely resembling human postures). On land, they give birth to their young or find shelter during the molt. While on land, though, these animals are usually very cautious. They always manage to find a location with quick access to water. Once safely back in the water, they regain their courage. Often they will allow an observer to come quite close. They will stare at the intruder, more curious than frightened.

For the harbor seal, a block of ice is always a good spot to rest. This species is also frequently encountered on sandy banks by river mouths and along sandy or rocky shores.

This map shows the distribution of the harbor seal along the western Atlantic coasts. The subspecies *Phoca vitulina concolor* dwells in these regions. Another subspecies, *Phoca vitulina vitulina*, lives on the coasts of northwestern Europe and on the British Isles. This latter species does not live in strictly icy regions. It tends to frequent areas where the waters are free from ice year round. It likes the estuaries and areas where the alternating tides break up the coastal ice. The size of the Canadian and American populations are more, or less, the same as that of the populations living on the European coasts. The American and Canadian seals have a light network of white stripes over their bluish gray coloring. This background is spotted with darker, almost black, marks. The underside is light, while the rest of the fur is tinted dark just like the seals of the British Isles.

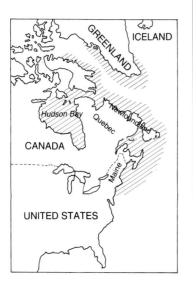

Four species of seals live in the North Atlantic. They are the harp seal, the hooded seal, the harbor seal, and the gray seal. The main reproduction areas of harp seals and hooded seals are in the Arctic. Both species come down to the northern part of Newfoundland and Labrador and to the Gulf of Saint Lawrence. They never reach the northern seas of western Europe. Their pups have magnificent fur. It is pure white in the harp seal with slate-blue on the back, plus light gray on the belly of the hooded seal. The pups of both species are hunted in Canada for their fur.

The other two species do not extend so far to the north. As a result, their pups do not need or have such a thick fur at birth. Seal pups' thick fur helps temperature regulation during their first month of life before their thermo-regulating system is functioning fully. The harbor seal and the gray seal are hunted only as adults, but not for their fur, which has no value on the market. Rather, they are hunted to limit the damage (real or presumed) that they cause to fishermen by feeding on commercially-important fish.

The harbor seal is easily distinguished from the gray seal. Its head is smaller and more rounded, and its nostrils are V-shaped with the lower tips almost touching. The males of this species can be 6 feet (1.8 m) in length, while the females are no longer than 5 feet (1.5 m).

Harbor seals mate from September to October while living in mixed social communities. At this time, the seals, which are normally rather quiet, give off long calls that sound like growls and yelps. Males engage in fights with much splashing of water. Sometimes in order to threaten their rivals, they suddenly leap upward and fall back with a loud thud. After mating, growth of the fertilized egg is held in check until November or December. This allows for pups to be born between May and June following a six-month pregnancy. Females pay close attention to the care of their young. They nurse them for four to six weeks, both on land and in the water, with milk particularly rich in fat.

In western Europe, seal hunting is strictly controlled today. It is permitted for most of the year, but not during the birth and nursing periods. Fortunately, the number of kills is very low. In North America up until 1976, seals were continuously hunted, with a bounty for each killed specimen. Today, ten years after the end of this mindless approach, seal populations are increasing at a very rapid rate.

The most common seal of the North Atlantic is probably not the harbor seal, but the gray seal. This species is

ICELAND

Faeroe Islands
Shetland Islands
The Hebrides
Orkney Island
North Sea

This map shows the European distribution of the harbor seal. About 200,000 reside along the British Isles. This is more than the entire population on the other side of the ocean. Another group of 30,000 is divided between Ireland and the coasts of continental Europe. Generally, these animals do not venture south of the Dutch coast, but they are often found along the French coast and sometimes even in Portugal. A small group also lives in the Baltic Sea. This seal does not regularly migrate like other species, but is nonetheless very mobile. After reproducing, the individuals scatter over a very wide territory. Some can even be found in inland waters along rivers that they will swim up for hundreds of miles. This habit may explain how a group of seals established the lake populations of some inland lakes of Canada. The lakes are separated from the ocean today. They are called "lakes of the seals" for the unusual guests they shelter.

harder to observe because it usually comes to land in more remote areas than the harbor seal. Moreover, gray seals never gather in large groups, except during the reproduction period.

Gray seals are larger than harbor seals. Males can reach 8 feet (2.4 m) in length, while females are a little more than 6 feet (2 m). This seal has a rather large head, resembling that of a horse. For this reason, fishermen in some regions call them "horse heads." This species lives only in the Atlantic Ocean. Its total population is about 135,000, half of which live along the British Isles.

Gray seals give birth later than harbor seals. The young are born between September and December in Great Britain, depending on the different colonies. Some births take place as late as January in Canada. The pups are nursed for only about three weeks. Then females let their young, which are already fairly independent, go their own way to deal with the males. At this time, males are already engaged in furious fights to form their harems, usually comprised of five to six females. The social structure of this species is very different from that of harbor seals and other similar species. Its behavior pattern is similar to, but not as extreme as, that of sea lions and hooded seals. Like the hooded seals, gray seals do not eat anything during the entire period of mating, delivery, and nursing. At the end of such a stressful reproduction season, they have lost considerable weight. Often in the more crowded colonies, the pups may be accidentally killed by the adult males. They are crushed to death in the fury of the males' fights.

In all the areas where gray seals live, fishermen consider them a serious threat to coastal fishing activities. Even today, in Canada, a bounty is given for each kill in an effort to reduce the numbers of this species. Seal hunting is forbidden only during the reproduction season from January to February. Seals are also hunted around the British Isles, especially on the Orkney and Shetland islands. There, also, hunting season is closed during the reproductive period from September through December.

The issue of seal hunting has long been debated, both at a scientific and a political level. On the one hand, most people consider this activity brutal and barbaric. On the other hand, fishermen maintain that this practice is necessary for their business to survive. They state it is necessary also, for the protection of the fish populations, which provide large quantities of food for human consumption.

The Cetaceans

The process of adaptation to life in the ocean has gone much farther with the cetaceans than with the pinnipeds. The tail of the cetacean is the main source of propulsion for the body and can also be used as a rudder. Unlike fish that have vertical, laterally moving tails, the cetaceans have horizontal tails which are moved up and down. Their hind legs have disappeared. Only the pelvic bones still exist in a rudimentary form. The front legs are modified into fins that are used for maneuvering and as stabilizers.

Unlike the pinnipeds, the cetaceans never return to land. They mate and give birth in the ocean. Unlike terrestrial mammals, pinniped young are born tail first, not head first. This adaptation eliminates the possibility that the newborn will drown as it comes out of its mother's body.

The gray seal dwells in more remote environments than the harbor seal. For this reason, it seems rarer than it actually is.

Soon after its birth, the mother or other group members push the newborn up to the surface for its first breath.

The mammary glands of the cetaceans are hidden inside the genital opening. As soon as the newborn touches the opening, a nipple will extend outward. Milk is pumped into the baby's mouth by the mother's muscles. The newborn babies are nursed on the surface so that they can breathe as they are eating. They will soon learn how to swim and how to feed under the water.

Water, as the Archimedes principle teaches, supplies an upward thrust. It provides a much greater push up than the air provides pushing down on any object immersed in it. For this reason, cetaceans do not need strong skeletal systems, such as those of terrestrial mammals, to support their weight. They have grown to a size that would be impossible for their skeletons to support if they lived on land. They are, in fact, much larger than the huge dinosaurs of the past. A large size is advantageous for many reasons. Foremost, is that it provides automatic protection against predators. On the other hand, it has some disadvantages. These animals require huge quantities of food to survive. They also cannot return to being land animals or ever dwell in shallow water. If they get stranded in the shallows, they may run aground. Their enormous weight can then crush their vital organs. Moreover, out of the water, they cannot easily dissipate the large quantities of heat their bodies normally give off through their skin.

The capacity of cetaceans to communicate with each other and to find their food under the water depends mainly on their ability to emit and to intercept sounds. This sophisticated hearing system, called "echo location" or "sonar," is hard for people to fully understand. These animals can actually "see" by means of this system. They perceive clear images the way modern sonar technology can record medical information. One example of such ultrasound is the "picture" that can be taken of the growing fetus when a pregnant woman is examined.

A Century of Persecution

Since the earliest times, people have hunted cetaceans. In fact, the flesh, fat, and bones of these animals are all commercially valuable. In the North Atlantic, whaling was first commercially organized as early as the eleventh century by Basque and Spanish fishermen in the Bay of Biscay. At that time, only right whales were hunted. These animals

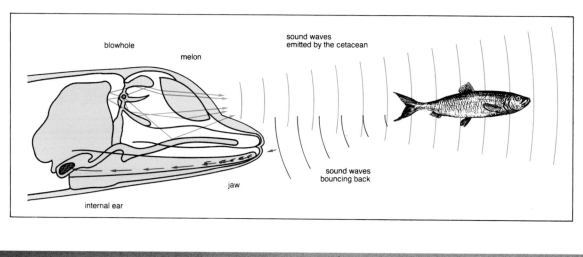

blowhole

melon

sound waves emitted by the cetacean

sound waves bouncing back

jaw

internal ear

were 50 to 60 feet (15 to 18 m) long and weighed up to fifty tons. They lived in groups of one hundred or more and fed on large herring schools.

By the end of the sixteenth century, the right whales were already rare along the coasts of Europe because of overhunting. The human population was constantly and rapidly increasing. Mineral oil was almost unknown at the time, and the demand for whale oil to be used for heating and light was very high. At first, right whale hunting shifted to the other side of the Atlantic Ocean off Newfoundland. In the seventeenth and eighteenth centuries, whaling fleets were constantly improving their hunting techniques. This was due mainly to the efforts of Dutch, English, and American whalers. They were forced to extend their search for their prey all the way to the Arctic and, in the process, increased their efficiency at the task.

In 1712, an American whaler named Christopher Hussey was fruitlessly looking for right whales when he was caught in a storm and drifted into the open sea. There he sighted and killed a sperm whale. In this way, immense reserves of spermaceti oil (1 to 5 tons for each individual) were discovered. Spermaceti is a waxy solid obtained from the oil of cetaceans and used in ointments, cosmetics, and candles. In the whale's body, spermaceti is found in an organ called the "melon," which is located in the forehead. This melon serves as a device somehow associated with diving or with the transmission of sounds. Since that time, the sperm whale has been relentlessly hunted all over the world. It provided prosperity to the harbor towns of New England and was made forever famous in Herman Melville's novel *Moby Dick.*

By the end of the nineteenth century, modern technology was growing rapidly in all fields. It was also being applied to the hunting of whales. Sailing ships were replaced by steamboats. The risky hand harpoon, which had to be thrown from a lightweight sloop, was replaced by the deadly cannon harpoon, shot directly from a large boat. As a consequence, the whale population plummeted. The first species to be affected was the blue whale, followed by the finback, and, finally, by the sei whale. This last species, smaller than the others, had until that time managed to escape the slaughter. At the beginning of the twentieth century, the whaling industry was still on the rise. Since the northern waters were already depleted, whalers moved into Antarctic waters. Since then, the whale populations have

The finback whale *(top)* and the right whale *(below)* are two relatively rare species in the North Atlantic. These two have different feeding patterns. The finback continually filters water through its baleen, trapping small planktonic crustaceans. The right whale chases schools of herring or other small fish and uses its filtering device only after it has stuffed prey into its large mouth.

remained small. In the last few years, however, due to strict rules on hunting imposed by international agreements, numbers seem to be slightly increasing.

Baleen Whales

Cetaceans are divided into two major groups—baleen whales and toothed whales. Baleen whales gather food by means of a peculiar outgrowth of the upper jaws called a "baleen." Toothed whales have actual teeth.

Many species of baleen whales are found in the North Atlantic. The most well known are the finback, the little piked or minke whale, and the humpback whale.

The jaws of these animals are very large and equipped with thin plates of baleen. Baleen is a horny material similar to fingernails that continually grows. Although they have a completely different origin than teeth, they may be considered functional equivalents. Teeth never grow in baleen cetaceans but are found in a primitive form in the embryos of these animals. Baleen plates are arranged in two rows that hang from the upper jaw on both sides of the mouth. The outer edge of each plate is smooth. Inside the mouth, each plate is fringed with hairlike bristles that form a dense filter. This highly-effective water filter traps plankton and small fish which form the diet of baleen cetaceans. A whale may have several hundred baleen. The finback, for example, has over nine hundred. They can be up to 35 inches (90 cm) long and 12 inches (30 cm) wide.

Usually, whales winter in warm waters at lower latitudes. Here they mate and give birth to their young. The minke whale winters south of Puerto Rico, while the humpback whale winters north of the Dominican Republic. It is not known for sure where the finbacks spend the winter. In the spring, all whale species migrate north. They head for the very rich waters off the coasts of New England, Newfoundland, and Labrador.

Two other species, less common than those just described, live on the western side of the Atlantic Ocean. These are the blue whale and the sei whale. Humpback whales are found all over the world. They are famous for their complex underwater vocalizations. They are made by the males in their reproduction areas to attract females. Among the most interesting audio recordings of such vocalizations are the *Songs of the Humpback Whales* and *Deep Voices*, both released by Capitol Records.

The other type of whale observed off the coasts of

In the mouth of this humpback whale, identified by its pock-marked skin, are the horny, layered baleen plates. The baleen cetaceans do not have teeth but are equipped, instead, with this kind of natural sifter. With it, they filter the water, trapping almost infinite numbers of microscopic prey. Their prey is incredibly small when compared to the whale's size. In order to survive, a whale must collect many tons of krill each year.

North America is the right whale. This cetacean has been strictly protected since 1937. As a result, its populations today are slowly but constantly growing. It seems that some biological factors have played a positive role in species such as the right whale that have suffered from human persecution. One of the effects of a decrease in the number of animals is a general increase in the female's fertility and earlier sexual maturity. Both changes may be considered positive. They favor a population growth that moves toward the original numbers. But it is unlikely that these levels will ever be reached again. This is because hunters are increasing their harvest of marine crustaceans called krill that are the main food of many species of whales.

Right whales, like all the other species mentioned so

The blue whale got its name because its skin has bluish gray spots. This species is rare in the North Atlantic Ocean.

far, are also baleen whales. Thus they, too, are equipped with plates and feed by filtering huge amounts of water. They migrate south for the winter and for the birth of their young. They are most easily observed from April to November off the coast of Maine.

Right whales and humpback whales are also known for their sudden and spectacular leaps out of the water. They seem to rotate on their tails in midair, then fall back into the water with a loud splash. This behavior, called "breaching,"

is considered by zoologists to be an important form of social communication. In fact, the sounds thus produced travel for very long distances under the water. It also may be a form of play.

The Toothed Whales: Dolphins, Porpoises, and Killer Whales

Toothed whales number many more species than baleen whales. In the North Atlantic, there are the large sperm whale, the bottle-nosed whale, the pilot whale, the killer whale, the harbor porpoise, the common dolphin, the white-sided dolphin, and the white-beaked dolphin. The sperm whale is the largest of the group at 59 feet (18 m) long. It is rarely seen close to the coast, as it prefers deep waters along the margins of the continental shelves. It hunts mainly large squid, diving much deeper for them than any other cetacean does. Its huge head, filled with spermaceti oil, is a special adaptation that allows this animal to dive to incredible depths. The oil acts as a flotation regulator. When the sperm whale dives, seawater flows through its nostrils, right into the middle of the spermaceti organ or melon. The oil cools down and becomes more dense. This makes the whale heavier and less capable of floating. Through this device, the sperm whale can regulate its density to match the waters in which it is hunting. Thus it can be in perfect equilibrium in the water, staying still and silent, waiting for the right moment to catch its prey. When it is time to surface, the sperm whale heats up its spermaceti by increasing the blood flow to the spermaceti organ.

The bottle-nosed whale is smaller than the sperm whale but can still grow from 23 to 29 feet (7 to 9 m) long. It is well known for its beaklike nose and protruding forehead. This was one of the last species to be hunted in the North Atlantic, especially by Norwegian, Icelandic, and Canadian whalers. About 28,000 whales were killed between 1965 and 1971. Their remains were made into cat and dog food or fed to minks on commercial fur-breeding farms. Bottle-nosed whale hunting was forbidden in 1972 when the populations of this species had been seriously reduced. The sentiment of the general public against whale hunting was very strong.

The small pilot whale, which grows from 10 to 20 feet (3 to 6 m), is among the most common of the medium-sized cetaceans in the North Atlantic. It is relatively easy to recognize. It has a glossy black coloration, bulbous head, and a

An obvious feature of the bottle-nosed whale is the protruding forehead, which contains the melon. This species can be 23 to 30 feet (7 to 9 m) long and weigh up to three tons.

large, highly-curved dorsal fin. Like sperm whales and bottle-nosed whales, pilot whales feed mainly on squid. They are always chasing squid schools and even migrate north with them during the summer. Usually these cetaceans live in groups of twenty or more. These gregarious habits make hunting for them easier. They are still hunted off the Faeroe Islands. There, fishermen surround the herds with several boats, making loud noises to scare the whales toward the coast. They beach themselves, which makes them easy prey. The stranding of these animals can also occur without the involvement of hunters. It can be accidental, caused by the highly sociable nature of this species. If one animal happens to find itself in water that is too shallow, it sends out a call of alarm. This attracts other members of the group that will then end up getting themselves stranded one after the other. Until a few years ago, people used to take advantage of such events to acquire considerable amounts of meat and fat. Today, however, in most countries, the local citizens gather to try to push the animals back into open water.

Another cetacean at times encountered in the Atlantic

Large cetaceans living in the Atlantic Ocean can be identified by the various heights and shapes of their blows and by their profiles when partially submerged. Moreover, some species lift their tails out of the water upon diving. The sperm whale, although as large as a baleen whale, belongs to the grouping of toothed whales.

Ocean is the magnificent killer whale. Its gigantic dorsal fin can be as high as 6 feet (1.8 m) or more. These are powerful predators, reaching lengths of 23 to 29 feet (7 to 9 m). They hunt as a group for fish, squid, birds, seals, porpoises, and even humpback whales and other whale species. Surprisingly enough, they do not attack humans, who would make very easy prey for them.

The smallest cetaceans, and also the easiest to see in the Atlantic, are the dolphins and the porpoises. The common dolphins, which grow to 6 feet (2 m) long, are swift swimmers. They will often jump out of the water and follow the wake of ships. Porpoises, which can be slightly smaller at 5 to 6 feet (1.5 to 1.8 m) long, are much shier. These animals, like many other species of the family, are well known for several traits. Their high sociability, their refined communication techniques, and their ability (with training) to communicate with humans make them especially appealing creatures.

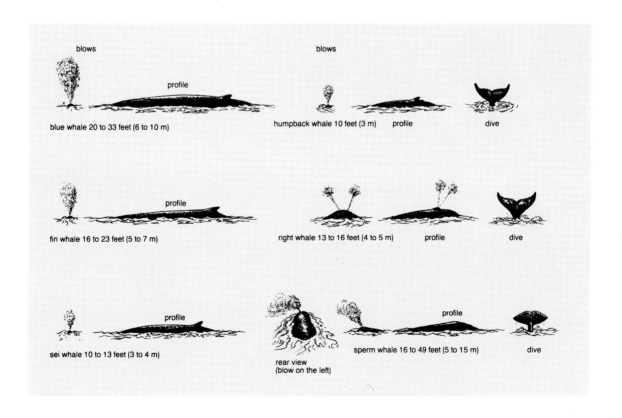

blows
profile
blue whale 20 to 33 feet (6 to 10 m)

blows
profile
dive
humpback whale 10 feet (3 m)

profile
fin whale 16 to 23 feet (5 to 7 m)

profile
dive
right whale 13 to 16 feet (4 to 5 m)

profile
sei whale 10 to 13 feet (3 to 4 m)

rear view
(blow on the left)

profile
dive
sperm whale 16 to 49 feet (5 to 15 m)

THE BRITISH ISLES

Among the many countries facing the Atlantic Ocean, the British Isles are exceptional for many reasons. They are located between 50 and 60 degrees north latitude. This puts them at the same latitude as Labrador or the southern point of Greenland. While the coasts of Labrador have an arctic climate, the British Isles, because of the influence of the Gulf Stream, have a maritime climate. In the southern reaches, the climate can be compared to that of Portugal. To the north, especially in the Scottish Highlands, the weather can display subarctic features. In comparison with continental Europe, the British Isles are colder and more humid in the summer and warmer in the winter. Moreover, due to the influence of the ocean, they are warmer and more humid in the western regions, colder and drier in the eastern.

Geological History

The landscape of the British Isles is highly varied. This is due, chiefly, to the complex geology of the land. The most ancient mountains, found in the Scottish Highlands and Northern Ireland, were formed over 600 million years ago during the Precambrian period. These are granite massifs (principal mountain masses) such as the Cairngorm Mountains in Scotland. Today, they are deeply eroded and smoothed. South of the Highlands, the areas of southern Scotland and southern Ireland, Wales, and most of England were covered by ocean waters for a long period of time. During millions of years, sand and silt accumulated on the ocean bottom. They were gradually compressed and formed layers of sedimentary rock, such as schist, limestone, and sandstone.

Around 350 million years ago, due to a violent lifting of the earth's crust, these rocks emerged from the water. They formed the huge mountain chain called the Caledonian Range. Today, only a few remnants of these mountains, once higher than Mount Everest, are left. They can be seen in the Lake District of England, in most of Wales, and in Cornwall a county in southwestern England.

Southeast of the Caledonian Range, the land underwent various cycles of lifting and settling. In different regions of England, therefore, sedimentary rock of different ages can be found. About 55 million years ago, major movements of the earth's crust that formed the Alps were also felt in southern England. The earth's crust buckled there, forming the low hills today known as the "Downs."

The English landscape has also been carved by a long

Opposite: This view is of the coast of Unst, one of the northernmost Shetland Islands. These approximately one hundred islands form an archipelago off the coast of Scotland.

About 18,000 years ago

About 11,000 years ago

About 8,000 years ago

During the last glaciation, about eighteen thousand years ago, the British Isles were connected to continental Europe. After the ice melted about eleven thousand years ago, the ocean level rose and Ireland became an island. Some small ice stretches remained on the Scottish Highlands. The last connection between France and England was flooded about eight thousand years ago. As the glaciers receded, the tundra, typical of the glacial front, was being replaced by birch and pine trees. Later on, when the climate became even milder, these trees were in turn replaced by hazelnuts, elms, and oaks. In the drawing, the ice cover is white. The areas with a mild climate are deep blue.

series of glacier activity during the last 250,000 years. The last glaciation reached its peak about eighteen thousand years ago. A glacier covered nearly all the surface of Great Britain, except for its southernmost regions, with an ice layer 8,202 feet (2,500 m) thick. At that time, due to the enormous quantity of water trapped in the form of ice, the ocean level was much lower than today. England was connected to the rest of Europe through a land bridge. What today is the North Sea used to be a wide depression covered with frozen tundra and swampy areas. Finally, a few thousand years ago, the ice melted and the ocean level rose. This caused the partial isolation of Great Britain from the European continent. The final separation occurred about 7,500 years ago with the formation of the English Channel. When the ice receded, the rainy, British maritime climate helped to establish forests over wide territories. Today, though, people have almost completely destroyed these primeval forests.

Pine and Birch Forests

Studies on pollen preserved in peat layers, show that about five thousand years ago, most of the British Isles were

Pictured is a view of the plains and hills of the Scottish Highlands. The original forest has all but disappeared from Great Britain. The hills of Scotland and other regions are now mainly covered by moors. The most common plant species of the moor is heather.

covered with a primeval "wild forest." It was very similar to the one that covered central Europe. In the Scottish Highlands, the main trees were pine and birch. In northern England, western Ireland, and in most of Wales, the most common trees were oak, hazelnut, basswood, and elm.

Observing the barren hills and moors of the present day Scottish Highlands, it is difficult to imagine that less than six hundred years ago these same areas were still covered by birch trees and scotch pines. They formed the ancient Caledonian Forest. Only a few patches of this forest are left today. They are mainly in northeastern Scotland along the shores of the Spey River. Where the pine forests are thin, there is underbrush with juniper plants and European mountain ash, a sturdy bush with red berries. Usually the ground is covered with heather, ferns, and black currants.

Wide areas of the Scottish Highlands and of the English plateaus have been replanted with commercially valuable trees such as conifer and larch (pine family). Many of these species are not native to the British Isles. Some that fall into this category are the maritime pine, the lodgepole pine, the

Often the English deciduous woods contain trees that are all the same age. The forests have either been invaded by grasses or suffer from depleted soils. This is the result of the management of the past decades. Woods were periodically cut down and often abandoned. Despite this, bright patches of color enliven the clearings. The picture shows the blossoming *Endymion non-scriptu.* The animal life of these woods is made up of small populations of many species.

red spruce, and a hybrid variety of larch, which results from crossing European larches and Japanese larches. These "artificial" forests lack diversity and are much more susceptible to insect damage. Lately, due to increasing pressure from conservationists and ecologists, a political climate has developed that may lead to the re-creation of a forest cover similar to the original.

Birch trees are also often found in the pine forests. The birch is a graceful-looking tree that, in spite of its frail appearance, is quite sturdy and can colonize infertile terrain. Its distribution area is not restricted to the Scottish Highlands. It extends over all the British Isles. It grows in poor and exposed soils where other more demanding trees cannot establish themselves. Two species of birch live on the British Isles. The common birch with drooping branches grows in the drier regions and on sandy or pebbly soils. The

white birch prefers wetter environments and is common on the western Scottish Highlands. It is often found clinging to boulders or rocky slopes, which are covered with green and yellow moss. Unlike the common birch, branches of the white birch do not droop. In addition, they are covered with soft hairs.

Deciduous Forests

Today, wide deciduous forests no longer exist on the English plains. Deciduous forests are comprised of deciduous trees, which are those that shed their leaves seasonally. None of the few remaining forests has been left untouched by society, either. For centuries, the deciduous forests have been exploited for the production of wood. Lumber is used for making fences, farming tools, and combustible material, and to produce wood coal. In order to harvest this kind of

The majestic look of old oak trees is deeply respected by the English people. They regard these trees as natural monuments. The trees are living memories of the forests that were destroyed in the previous centuries.

wood, young plants are cut back at the base. This encourages a rapid regrowth of new shoots. Somewhere between eight and twenty years, the trees are cut again and a new cycle begins. At first, an open type of habitat exists in the forest. Gradually the wood grows thick and the trees produce shade. Quite often, spectacular blossoms of primrose, violets, orchids, wood anemones, and bellflowers grow alongside the cuts in the wood. After a few years, these delicate flowers are choked out by brambles. Thick woods emerge where songbirds like the blackcap, the whitethroat, and the garden warbler can nest.

In England, the exploitation of the woods through this

cutting technique began to decline in the early 1920s. Today, many of these woods are abandoned. They are very shady and are home to a number of bird species. Other woods have been uprooted and turned into farmland or replanted with exotic commercial conifers. Only a few patches of the ancient forest are still intact. Today, they are protected as natural parks or reserves.

Of the native deciduous trees, ash, beech, and oak can still be found. Typical plants of the shrub layer are the hazelnut, the cornel tree (dogwood), the hawthorn and the bourtree (black-fruited elder). The most typical species of the grass layer are the fumitory (common European hub), the bellflower, the wood anemone, and the catchfly.

The beech, with its smooth and slender gray trunk, creates an ancient, cathedral-like atmosphere in the forest. It is found all over the British Isles. It is especially common in the southeastern regions where the climate is milder and less rainy. Its dense canopy completely shades the ground, hindering the growth of underlying vegetation.

Oaks are among the most common English trees. There are two main species. *Quercus peduncolata* is more common in the fertile plains. *Quercus sessilis* is found at higher elevations on acidic soils. Oak groves are a rich and complex environment. When fully developed, they show marked horizontal layers of vegetation. In spring, when the oaks are still leafless, the forest ground becomes covered with tetterwort, primrose, and wood anemones. After the first leaves appear on trees, all the shade-loving plants blossom. These include ground ivy, broad-leafed garlic, spurges, and bellflowers. In the bushy layer are hazelnuts, hawthorns, and thornbushes. All of these shrubs form a good environment for the nesting of blackbirds, black-capped chickadees, garden warblers, and jays. The jays play a very important role in the spread of the oak trees. They bury acorns in hideaways, storing them for the winter. Some of them are forgotten and sprout the following spring.

Prairies, Moors, and Heaths

For centuries, these regions have suffered the effects of grazing by deer, cattle, sheep, and goats. As a result, heaths and moors have developed in the southern regions of England. In the western and northern regions, heaths predominate. The distinction between heaths and moors is not always clear. Generally, the soil of heaths is sandy and pebbly, while that of moors is peaty (made of carbonized

vegetable tissues). In both cases, though, the main plants are heather and ling. Normally these plants cannot live on alkaline soils. When the woods are cut down in an alkaline area, prairies take over.

The grassy plateaus of southern England are called the "Downs." The soil is light there, well drained, and infertile. In fact, some essential minerals like phosphorus, nitrogen, potassium, and iron are lacking. The most common plants are quaking grass, whose fragile stems quiver in the lightest breeze, the aromatic wild thyme, and vetch. The Downs are famous for their orchids. In June, some slopes are literally carpeted with rose-colored, scented, pyramid-like spikes of flowers. Orchids grow slowly. Many years may pass before they blossom for the first time. This rich plant life forms the habitat for some of the most graceful English butterflies. Due to a lack of surface water, though, bird species are limited. The most typical of this environment are meadow pipits, larks, lapwings, and kestrels.

The typical appearance of the Downs is dry. They are subject to continuous grazing, mainly by sheep and rabbits. In recent years, though, raising sheep on these hills has almost completely stopped. The rabbit population has been decreasing as well, following the introduction in 1953 of myxomatosis virus which is a highly contagious lethal virus that affects rabbits and hares. As a result, wide stretches of the Downs today are invaded by shrubby plants, mainly junipers, and are slowly turning back into woods.

The plateaus of the British Isles that have poor drainage and are, therefore, wetter look like barren moors covered with peat. The soil is acidic and poor in nutrients. It is especially lacking in calcium. Deer, alpine hares, and voles find plenty of food on these plateaus. In the wettest areas, redshanks and snipes are particularly common birds. In the drier prairies, on the other hand, there are lapwings, larks, meadow pipits, curlews, and golden plovers. Predator mammals include the fox, the ermine, and the weasel. Among the predator birds, the most important are the merlin, the hen harrier, and even the golden eagle. The golden eagles number three hundred pair in Great Britain. They live in Scotland.

Insects abound on the southern heaths. They provide plenty of food for many small animals. In these areas, all six species of reptiles existing in Great Britain can be found. They are the blindworm (a lizard), the viviparous (producing living young instead of eggs) lizard, the sandlizard, the

Typical plants of the moors are *Erica cinerea,* which is found on the dry moors, and *Erica tetralix,* which is found on wetter ground.

Erica cinerea

Erica tetralix

collared lizard, smooth snake, and the viper. The viper is the only poisonous snake on the British Isles. It preys on lizards, voles, and shrews. It tracks down its prey by sampling the soil with its tongue. That is where its sense of smell is located.

When water is plentiful, the moor takes on a new look. In the valleys where a great deal of water collects, peat starts accumulating. The so-called valley bogs are formed in this manner. Numerous plant species typical of swamps such as the swamp asphodel (perennial hub of the lily family), *Myrica gale,* and *Drosera rotundifolia* are also found. The latter is an insect-eating plant. It acquires the nitrogen necessary for its growth by trapping and digesting any insect that lands on its sticky, spoon-shaped leaves. The swamp asphodel is a little lily with spikes of yellow flowers. It is also called the "bone-breaker." In the past it was incorrectly believed to cause the bones of cattle or sheep that fed upon it to become brittle.

Some moors are covered by nard, a plant which is too tough to provide good grazing. Yet another type of moor where heather is the main species gives shelter to the Scottish white ptarmigan and to deer. Heather grows in thick mats, mostly in the eastern, drier areas at higher elevations. In late summer when the heather blossoms, the area is covered by a unique purple carpet. It offers a truly brilliant show. Besides heather, black and red currants, bearberries, cineraria, and other plant species abound.

On many moors, the vegetation is managed in a way that will increase the number of the white Scottish ptarmigans. These birds are in high demand and are considered a valuable catch by hunters. The white Scottish ptarmigan lives only on the British Isles, but it is not a true species. It is a subspecies of the willow ptarmigan, which is widespread in subarctic moors all over the world. One of the main differences between these two birds is that the Scottish ptarmigan does not have white winter plumage. Due to the maritime climate of the British Isles, the Scottish Highlands are not covered with snow in winter. Thus the Scottish ptarmigan does not need to take on white coloration the way the willow ptarmigan does.

Hedges

A special characteristic of farmed land on the plains of the British Isles are the hedges surrounding the small fields. They give a checkerboard appearance to the landscape.

Farming has thoroughly changed the English landscape. Throughout this land, however, there is still more room for wild animals than in other European countries. Hedges that separate the fields are an ideal environment for many species of birds and small mammals.

From an ecological viewpoint, these hedges are comparable to the area along the edges of the woods. They are arranged, however, in more or less straight lines. Hedges are an important habitat for the animals and plants typical of the plains.

Hedges also provide protection as well as housing for many birds such as blackbirds, hedge sparrows, and robins. If the hedges border a meadow, pheasants, partridges, and corn buntings also inhabit them. Small rodents, like voles and long-tailed field mice, dwell in burrows dug in the ground. They feed on hawthorn berries and other fruit provided by hedge plants. At the base of the bushes, tiny shrews are always on the move looking for small invertebrates. At night, hedgehogs come out in search of snails, beetles, and the larvae of insects and worms.

Unfortunately, the abundant life-forms of this specialized habitat are seriously threatened today. The use of farm machinery requires wide open spaces, so many hedges have been uprooted. This has caused the loss of large numbers of animals as well as the flattening of a landscape that has been famous for centuries.

GUIDE TO AREAS OF NATURAL INTEREST

A visit to the reserves and national parks that face the Atlantic Ocean is an easy and deeply-satisfying experience. The roads are usually good. Boat connections are regular to the various locations, at least during good weather. Hotels and restaurants are affordable. Naturalist literature on these areas is rich and exhaustive. There are guidebooks on every conceivable topic. Some are birds, flowering plants, butterflies, insects, mushrooms, ferns, mosses, reptiles, amphibians, mammals, sea animals, domestic animals, types of soil, rocks, and even grasses. These areas are an ideal spot for scholars of seals and seabirds. They are also especially suited for anyone who likes to travel in an organized way with events scheduled in advance.

Usually, the small islands where seabirds nest can be visited by boat. No special equipment is necessary for such visits apart from a good raincoat as protection from the splashing of the waves. On the trails, the usual rules are to be remembered. They include bringing boots if the ground is swampy, a small backpack with some food and beverages, and binoculars (eight to ten times magnification) if birdwatching is planned. Besides a good camera, a tape recorder will also prove useful. The loud and engaging sounds of the coast can then be captured. These include the wind blowing and the waves crashing on the rocks, and the loud calls of seabirds. Sometimes, the siren of a boat or the voice of a guide from a loudspeaker telling a group of tourists all about the behavior of solan geese can be heard.

It is possible to alternate excursions in the parks and reserves with visits to museums, libraries, monuments, and other attractions. The best period for this kind of tourism is in the spring and summer beginning in May. As far as the seabird colonies go, after the first two weeks of July, guillemots and puffins usually go back to the open sea. Only cormorants, gannets, and gulls are still on their nests. It is unlikely, even in the warmest years, that the weather will be warm enough to allow a swim in the ocean. The waters, in fact, always stay quite cold. Even when the sun has been shining for many days, swimming is not very enjoyable.

In midsummer, the Atlantic climate can be less than inviting. Sudden showers can arise. Luckily they are usually short-lived. Nevertheless, a sunny day spent on a black volcanic island surrounded by deep blue sea and sky is an experience that no rain shower can spoil. The land is carpeted with emerald grass and purple stretches of heather, and seabirds are all around.

Opposite: The lighthouse is found on Cape Hatteras in North Carolina. This region of North Carolina hosts a national seashore.

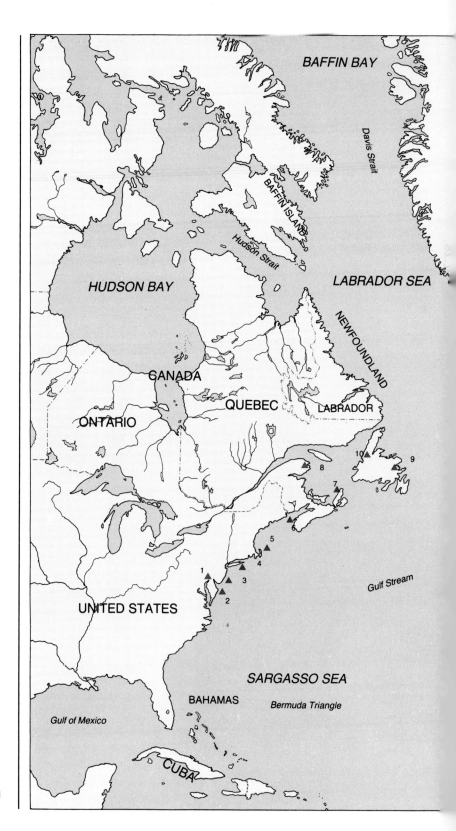

Shown is the North Atlantic Ocean, with the North American, North African, and European coasts. The islands and major areas of natural interest are noted throughout.

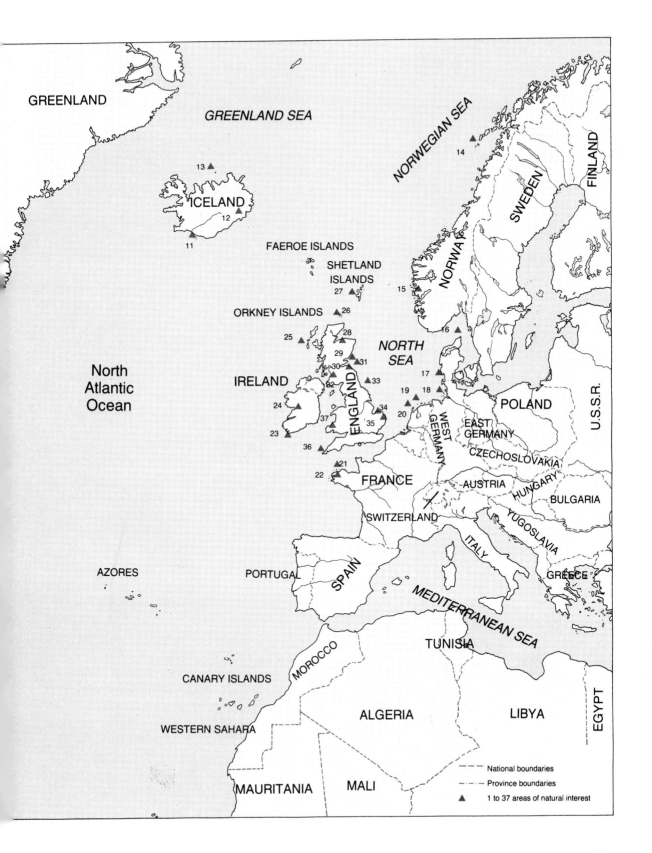

GREENLAND

GREENLAND SEA

NORWEGIAN SEA

14 ▲

ICELAND

13 ▲

12

11

FAEROE ISLANDS

SHETLAND
ISLANDS

27 ▲ ▲

15

ORKNEY ISLANDS ▲ 26

25 ▲

28 ▲

NORTH
SEA

16 ▲

North
Atlantic
Ocean

IRELAND

29 ▲
30 ▲ ▲ 31
32

33 ▲

17 ▲

19 18
▲ ▲

24 ▲

34 ▲

20

37 ▲
35 ▲

23 ▲

36 ▲

21 ▲
22

FRANCE

SWITZERLAND

SWEDEN

NORWAY

FINLAND

POLAND

EAST
GERMANY

WEST
GERMANY

CZECHOSLOVAKIA

AUSTRIA

HUNGARY

BULGARIA

YUGOSLAVIA

ITALY

GREECE

U.S.S.R.

AZORES

PORTUGAL

SPAIN

MEDITERRANEAN SEA

CANARY ISLANDS

MOROCCO

TUNISIA

EGYPT

WESTERN SAHARA

ALGERIA

LIBYA

MAURITANIA

MALI

- - - - National boundaries
- · - · Province boundaries
▲ 1 to 37 areas of natural interest

107

UNITED STATES

Maryland:
Blackwater (1)

Delaware:
Bombay Hook (2)

New Jersey:
Brigantine (3)

New York:
Fire Island (4)

Massachusetts:
Cape Cod (5)

This National Wildlife Refuge is 17 sq. miles (45.4 sq. km). It is an important wintering area for the water birds that migrate along the Atlantic route. It is located around Chesapeake Bay and includes bushy areas, swampy woods of pine and red maple, freshwater marshes, and ponds.

The mammals include muskrats, raccoons, opossums, skunks, otters, and squirrels. As for birds, there are various grebes, ospreys, gallinules, killdeer plovers, and several species of ducks and geese.

This is a national wildlife refuge, 2 sq. miles (6 sq. km). It includes the swampy marshes of an estuary in the Delaware Bay, as well as freshwater ponds and swampy woods.

This area is also an important wintering and nesting site for the water birds that migrate along the Atlantic routes. Among the species nesting here are the Canada goose, various ducks and herons, and many forest birds. The refuge has an observation tower and can be crossed by a well-maintained gravel road.

This national wildlife refuge is 30 sq. miles (78.6 sq. km). It includes marshes and also tidal bays on the Atlantic coast north of Atlantic City.

Inland, some freshwater pools offer a perfect habitat to over 150,000 birds. They stop to nest or to rest during their migrations. The most common species seen are skimmers, several rails (wading birds), terns, gulls, ducks, and geese. The mammals include white-tailed deer, skunks, opossums, mink, muskrats, and, squirrels.

This national seashore, 2 sq. miles (5.7 sq. km), is part of a barrier island a little south of Long Island. The New York skyline is almost in sight. It is a wilderness area, accessible only on foot. It offers brackish swamps and forests with sassafras and other plant species.

The beautiful monarch butterflies can be observed here on pine branches. Among the birds, there are herons, ducks, geese, and terns. The sea teems with mackerel and other species of open-water fish. The famous horseshoe crabs also live in this area.

Cape Cod is a vast deposit of glacial materials at the southernmost limits of the last glaciation period. The national seashore here is 22 sq. miles (57 sq. km) wide and includes wide expanses of sandy coasts and sand dunes.

Most of the coastline faces the open Atlantic. The stretch between Truro and Wellfleet faces the waters of Cape Cod Bay. Coastal erosion is very rapid. The shore is worn away at the rate of about 3 feet (1 m) per year. The habitats in this area are very rich and varied. There are freshwater pools and brackish swamps as well as maple and pine woods.

The park is an important wintering area for large flocks of eider ducks, velvet scoters, Canada geese, and black ducks. Among the birds of prey are the Cooper's hawks, the red-tailed hawks, and the hen harriers. Mammals include rabbits, foxes, white-tailed deer, skunks, muskrats, and otters. The peculiar horseshoe crabs are often found on the beach. Between the rocks, both gastropods and bivalve mollusks are abundant.

UNITED STATES /CANADA

Eastern North American Coast (6)

Observing whales in the open sea is a common hobby on the eastern coast of North America. It is also possible to watch these animals from land. There are many good observation points in the area. During the summer, humpback whales and other whale species come close to the coast. Their food, small crustaceans and fish, is abundant there.

In Newfoundland, the best places to watch for whales are at Cape Race, on the cliffs of Bay de Verde in Conception Bay, at Trinity Bay, at Cape Bonavista by Elleston, and at the lighthouse of Cape St. Mary in Placentia Bay.

There are other good places to watch for whales and, in summer, also belugas (white sturgeons). One is the lighthouse at Forillon National Park, which is close to the town of Gaspé in southeastern Quebec. Another is off the high cliffs close to Les Escoumins and Tadoussac, also in Quebec, and on the Saint Lawrence River.

In New Brunswick, the best observation points are the Swallowtail lighthouse on the Grand Manan Island at the entrance to the Bay of Fundy, and the Head Harbor lighthouse on Campobello Island. In Maine, there is good "whale watching" along the high cliffs of West Quoddy Head State Park close to Lubec in the northeast corner of the state. The Bass Harbor lighthouse on Mount Desert Island off the southern coast of Maine is another good place. On the dunes of Cape Cod, especially close to Provincetown, Truro, and Wellfleet are the spots in Massachusetts.

If planning open-sea excursions, many whale-watching expeditions are available, especially off the coast of Maine and off the northern shores of the Saint Lawrence River by the mouth of the Saguenay River. There are many organizations dealing with such expeditions.

CANADA

Nova Scotia:
Cape Breton Highlands (7)

This national park, 324 sq. miles (840 sq. km), straddles the northern part of Cape Breton Island. It stretches all the way to the Gulf of Saint Lawrence. There are rocky shores on its eastern side with promontories of pink or gray granite, sandy inlets, and long stretches of cliffs. Inland there is a wide plateau with signs of ancient glaciers. Today, it is covered by a magnificent forest.

Among the mammals are the black bear, the white-tailed deer, the lynx, the snowshoe hare, the marten, the otter, the mink, the moose, and the chipmunk.

Quebec: Forillon (8)

This national park, covering 92 sq. miles (238 sq. km), is located on the tip of the Gaspé Peninsula, between the Gulf of Saint Lawrence and the Gaspé Bay. Jagged, sandstone cliffs make up most of the coastline. The cliffs alternate with small sandy or pebbly beaches. Many brooks and streams flow into the ocean in this area, often with rapids or waterfalls.

Many times, groups of seals will rest on the cliffs off the coast. Sometimes whales can be sighted from Cape Forillon. Over 220 species of birds have been reported in this area. A few miles south of the park nests the largest colony of solan geese in North America.

Newfoundland:
Terra Nova (9)

This national park stretches for 153 sq. miles (396 sq. km) along the Atlantic coast northwest of St. John's in Newfoundland. It also includes part of the inland territories along the coasts of a stupendous fjord, the Newman Sound. This area offers a remarkable variety of habitats. There are islands with many birds, areas of peat moss, lakes, forests, and mountains.

The waters here teem with fish (tuna among other species). They are visited by a great many seabirds. There are harp seals, several species of whales, and giant squid. The most extraordinary feature of the park, though, is its "parade" of icebergs. In the summer, they flow slowly by heading south, carried by the Labrador Current.

Inland, peat moss provides the ideal habitat for some delicate orchids, like the dragon's tongue and the *Listera sp.*, with its large blossoms. Carnivorous species are found here. One is the so-called pitcher plant, with its leaves modified into pitchers (in this case, insect-trapping). Further inland, *Pyrala sp.*, *Myrica sp.*, and Linnea are replaced by shrubs with beautiful blossoms. Then the real forests start. In this environment are found moose, bear, and lynx.

Newfoundland: Gros Morne (10)

This is the most spectacular part of the Long Range Mountains on the western coast of Newfoundland. It is a national park, 749 sq. miles (1,941 sq. km). In this area are signs of ancient glaciation. There are glacial valleys, lakes shaped like fjords, and moraines, which are accumulations of earth and stones carried and deposited by glaciers.

The park includes 107 miles (172.4 km) of coastline with sheer cliffs above the sea, silt or sand flats, and rocky shores. Marine fauna abounds in these environments. A great many migratory shorebirds find shelter on the silt flats. Among the species which nest on the coastal plains are the spotted sandpiper, the semipalmated plover, and the greater yellowlegs. Alpine hares, bald eagles, and ospreys are encountered on the mountains.

ICELAND

Westman (11)

The Westman Islands are located off the southern coast of Iceland. They are one of the most important European reproduction sites for seabirds. These islands consist of about twenty volcanic land masses. Heimaey, 3 miles (5 km) long, is the only one large enough to host a village.

Among the birds that nest here are cormorants, green cormorants, Mediterranean shearwaters, storm petrels, fulmars, foolish guillemots, Brünnich's guillemots, black guillemots, razorbills, glaucous gulls, kittiwakes, skuas, and puffins. Heimaey Island can be reached by boat or by plane from Reykjavik, or by boat from Stokkseyri.

Skaftafell (12)

This national park is located on the southeastern coast of Iceland and is 1,930 sq. miles (5,000 sq. km). It is famous for its breathtaking views of glaciers, waterfalls, gorges, hot springs, and a large sandy plain. The mountain slopes, up to 853 feet (260 m) in elevation, are covered by forests of small birch trees. Lower down, there are wood geraniums, bellflowers, wild angelica, yellow bedstraw, and other flora.

This area is well known for its nesting colonies of skuas, arctic skuas, and great black-backed gulls. The park is open June 1 through September 15 and offers good trails and well-equipped campgrounds.

Grimsey (13)

This island is located off the northern coast of Iceland within the Arctic Circle. It is about 2 miles (4 km) long and about 1 mile (2 km) wide. Thirty-six species of birds nest here. They include foolish guillemots and Brünnich's guillemots, razorbills, puffins, kittiwakes, fulmars, red-necked phalaropes, snow buntings, and ravens.

NORWAY

Lofoten (14)

The Lofoten Islands, while rocky and jagged, are covered with green pastures. This makes them a favorite spot for bird-watchers. In fact, about five million seabirds nest here. Among them are puffins, foolish guillemots, black guillemots, kittiwakes, storm petrels, fulmars, eider ducks, terns, arctic skuas, curlews, red-necked phalaropes, white-tailed eagles, and others. Röst, the main island, is reached by boat from Vest-Lofoten or directly from Bod. Bod in turn is connected with Oslo by trains and planes.

Vestlandet (15)

The fjords of Vestlandet were created some one thousand years ago by the action of glaciers. Sogne Fjord, one of the largest, is 124 miles (200 km) long and averages 2,625 feet (800 m) in depth. The glacier that created this fjord still exists today inland, but it is very small. North of Sogne Fjord is Jostedalstre. At 480 sq. miles (1,243 sq. km), it is the largest glacier in Europe. Past Odda is the Folgefonn glacier, 108 sq. miles (280 sq. km) wide.

Off these fjords, a great many little islands form the ideal shelter for many nesting seabirds. Runde is one of these, especially well known to bird-watchers. It is easily reached by boat from Alesund. The most common bird species are the kittiwake and the puffin, but bald eagles, horned owls, and duck hawks also live there. Vestlandet offers good tourist facilities. There are fjord excursion boats, campgrounds, and hotels.

DENMARK

Skagen (16)

When the glaciers of the Quaternary period receded for the last time, sea sediments, freed from the huge weight of the ice masses, rose and formed the wide stretches of sand typical of the Danish coast. An example of this kind of habitat is the nature reserve of Skagen, 17 sq. miles (43 sq. km). It is a narrow peninsula of sandy deposits located at the northern tip of Denmark. Particularly interesting are the many different kinds of fine-sand dunes and the shores covered with smooth pebbles. The reserve is an ideal loca-

Romo (17)

tion for watching migratory birds, especially from early April to early June. It offers a bird observatory and a campground. Access to the reserve is free.

This natural park is an island 47 sq. miles (121 sq. km) off the southwestern coast of Denmark. It is connected to the mainland by a road built above the water level. Its coasts are dominated by large sand dunes and tidal mud flats. Its interior is made up of large, seasonal swamps.

Reedy and marshy areas provide a good habitat for the marsh hawk and Montagu's harrier. Ducks and shorebirds stop on the mud flats. Among them are teals and shovelers, golden plovers, avocets, whimbrels (curlews), and redlegs. Access to the area is from Skaerback and is free.

WEST GERMANY

Ostfriesische
Wattenmeer and Dollart (18)

This is a wetland of international interest. It includes a chain of small, sandy islands, the East Frisians, as well as 10 to 12 miles (16 to 20 km) of sand and mud flats. These flats stretch between the islands and the northern coast of continental Germany.

This is an important stopping point for a great many ducks, geese, and migratory shorebirds. Among the species nesting here are the sheldrakes, curlews, oystercatchers, terns, eider ducks, redlegs, black-tailed godwits, and numerous types of gulls.

Access to Dollart is by boat from Emden, while the other islands can be reached from Norden. A permit is necessary to visit most of the areas of greatest interest.

HOLLAND (THE NETHERLANDS)

Terschelling (19)

This is the second largest of the West Frisian Islands. It is mainly covered with brackish swamps, meadows, brush, and sand dunes. On the island are three nature reserves: Koegelwek, 1 sq. mile (2.5 sq. km), Noodvaader, 25 sq. miles (65 sq. km), and Boschplaat, 17 sq. miles (44 sq. km).

The vegetation is rich and varied. It includes some pioneer species, such as *Salicornia europea* (growing in the brackish swamps), sedges, and other small plants on the higher parts of the sandy stretches. Also on the dunes are the sea buckthorn, poverty grass, orchids, swamp gentian, and others.

There are numerous bird species living in the area including a colony of spoonbills. Access is by boat from Harlingen.

In this charming view of an Icelandic landscape, a rainbow arches over a volcanic peak. Fishing boats sit, ready to be launched.

Texel (20)

Texel is the southernmost West Frisian island. Located 50 miles (80 km) north of Amsterdam, it is 9 miles (15 km) long and 7 miles (11 km) wide. It includes nineteen bird reserves and is one of the most interesting natural areas in all of Europe. It offers a variety of habitats. There are sand dunes, prairies, swamps, and mixed forests. Among the many birds nesting here are colonies of spoonbills, avocets, black-tailed godwits, marsh hawks, Montagu's harriers, bitterns, ducks, gulls, various species of terns, shorebirds, and passerines.

FRANCE

Les Sept Iles (21)

This small nature reserve includes a group of islands about 4 miles (7 km) off the northeastern coast of Brittany.

These islands are the northernmost site of reproduction for puffins, gannets, and fulmars in Europe. Among the seabirds are the kittiwakes, razorbills, herring gulls, common gulls, and great black-backed gulls.

Access to the islands is from Perros-Guirec. Daily boat excursions are organized from there during the summer for bird-watching.

Armorica (22)

This national park, which is 403 miles (650 km) long, is the largest protected area in Brittany. It includes varied habitats: moors, swamps, small fields, brushes, and little sea islands. Especially interesting are colonies of gray seals and harbor seals living on the Ouessant Isle. Access to the area is from Brest, Morlaix, or Quimper. The nature trails are in very good condition.

IRELAND

Cape Clear (23)

Cape Clear, located in the extreme southwestern part of Ireland, has a bird observatory that was built in 1959 by a group of bird lovers. In the fall there, it is possible to watch huge numbers of migrating birds, often gathered in large groups.

Shearwaters, storm petrels, fulmars, gannets, skuas, gulls, terns, sea ducks, and auks fly over the area. Moreover, black guillemots and Cornish choughs (Old World crows) nest on the island. Numerous migratory passerines also stop by to rest.

The Burren (24)

This area, located on the western coast of Ireland, is among the best on the British Isles for observing the effect of the Gulf Stream on vegetation.

It is a region of limestone cliffs rising high above Galway Bay, at the same latitude as southern Labrador. In spite of this, frost in winter is a rare occurrence. The humid winds coming from the ocean allow for the growth of lush vegetation. Mosses, lichens, hepaticas, and ferns can be found. The flowering plants are a peculiar blend of a Nordic species left behind by glaciation. Some species are from warmer areas. One of these is the madrone, which is a type of evergreen.

UNITED KINGDOM

**Scotland:
Balranald (25)**

This is a coastal nature reserve, 2 sq. miles (6 sq. km), on North Uist Island in the outer Hebrides. It protects a typical grassy habitat, very fertile and full of flowers locally called "machair." Among the flowering plants are the orchid, the wild thyme, the eyebright (an herb), and the field gentian.

The area attracts large numbers of shorebirds. Some that nest here are the lapwing, the redleg, the oystercatcher, the snipe, the dunlin, the arctic tern, the little tern, as well as eight species of ducks. The special attraction of this reserve is a small group of corncrakes, which are birds of the rail group, that are almost extinct in Great Britain today.

**Scotland:
North Hoy (26)**

This is one of the eight reserves owned by the Royal Society for the Protection of Birds on the Orkney Islands. It is comprised of a group of hills covered with moors and sloping down all the way to the sea. At that point, it ends in spectacular, high cliffs. This area has come to be known as "The Old Man of Hoy."

The most common bird species here is the fulmar. Many others are there, including green cormorants, kittiwakes, guillemots, razorbills, skuas, duck hawks, merlins, kestrels, hen harriers, red-throated divers, golden plovers, water-pipits, and whitetails. Among the mammals, the hare is especially common. Due to the strong winds, the vegetation is often dwarfed and twisted.

The island can be reached by boat from Stromness at Moness Pier, or from Outon at Lyness.

**Scotland:
Shetland (27)**

The Shetland Islands are at the northernmost point of the British Isles, at 60 degrees north latitude. They host four nature reserves, intended mainly to protect the numerous seabirds. One reserve is located on the northwestern tip of Unst, the northernmost island. Two others are on Fetlar Island and on the Isle of Noss. The last is on Ronas Hill on the large Mainland Island. All in all, these reserves cover about one-tenth of the total surface area of the archipelago, which covers 560 sq. miles (1,450 sq. km). Along the coast, rocky stretches alternate with narrow fjords. Almost 200,000 pairs of puffins reproduce there. The pebbly and rocky shores, on the other hand, are the favorite resting spot for gray seals and harbor seals to reproduce. Some rare and unexpected sandy beaches also occur. Especially on the smaller islands, otters, grebes, and shorebirds are found. A bird observatory was built on Fair Isle in 1948, and its staff has recorded the presence, constant or occasional, of over three hundred species of birds.

Inland on the larger island, there are interesting archeological remains predating Celtic and Norman colonizations. Shetland sheep, well known for their valuable wool, also abound here. The islands are accessible by plane or boat from Aberdeen.

Scotland: Loch Garten (28)

This reserve, 3 sq. miles (9 sq. km), is located in the Scottish Highlands. It was created to preserve some remains of the pine forests that once covered most of Scotland. It also contains some stretches of moorland and farmland. Various species of birds typical of the conifer forests inhabit this reserve. Among them are the wood grouse, the black grouse, the coal titmouse, the treecreeper, the firecrest, the crested tit, and the Scottish crossbill. Of special interest, besides the Scottish crossbill, is the osprey. It has come back to nest here after an absence of many years.

In spring, the lake waters attract many ducks and geese. Moreover, the woods are inhabited by deer, roe deer, squirrels, badgers, foxes, and even wildcats.

The reserve is located along a small road between the villages of Boat of Garten and Nethy Bridge.

Scotland: Isle of May (29)

This small island is located inside the Firth of Forth (the fjord on which Edinburgh is located). It is only 0.2 sq. miles (0.5 sq. km) yet it gives shelter to numerous colonies of seabirds. These include fulmars, green cormorants, kittiwakes, guillemots, razorbills, and puffins. This island is an important stopover point for the migratory birds.

Scotland: Bass Rock (30)

This spectacular, jagged little island is located off of North Berwick in the southern part of the Firth of Forth. Here thousands of pairs of gannets, fulmars, green cormorants, guillemots, kittiwakes, razorbills, and others come to nest.

118

The island can be seen from the sea during a boat tour that leaves from North Berwick throughout the summer.

England: Farne (31)

This is a group of small, rocky and barren islands, 1 sq. mile (3 sq. km) in all. It lies off the coast of northeastern England, teeming with colonies of seabirds. There are puffins, guillemots, razorbills, cormorants, green cormorants, oystercatchers, fulmars, terns, eider ducks, and kittiwakes. Also, a large colony of gray seals lives there.

England: Lake District (32)

This is the largest and the most well-known English national park. Covering 880 sq. miles (2,280 sq. km), this park includes a great variety of habitats. There are mountains, lakes, pools, streams, woods, and coastal dunes.

The most common birds dwelling in the wetlands are curlews, golden plovers, and sandpipers. The woods give shelter to many small birds of the passerine, or perching songbirds group. There are mammals such as squirrels, deer, roe deer, badgers, otters, and martens as well.

England: Bempton Cliffs (33)

The Bempton Cliffs, close to Flamborough Head, offer the chance to watch a spectacular grouping of seabirds. The cliffs are conveniently located along the coast and easily accessible.

England: Snettisham (34)

This reserve is 5 sq. miles (13 sq. km) and is located in the county of Norfolk along the eastern coast of The Wash. It covers tidal beds, brackish swamps, lagoons, and beaches.

In winter, about 70,000 birds gather on the silt flats. There are black-bellied plovers, knots, bar-tailed godwits, oystercatchers, dunlins, redlegs, turnstones, curlews, sanderlings, sheldrakes, brants, small geese, and wild geese. The vegetation is also very rich inside the reserve, providing many places for hiding or nesting.

England: Minsmere (35)

This is a famous reserve for birds that stretches 2 sq. miles (6 sq. km) along the eastern coast of Suffolk. Its main habitat is provided by the reeds. Bitterns, water rails, kingfishers, marsh hawks, and many other species live there. In the surrounding woods are woodpeckers and forest passerines. Many shorebirds, first and foremost the avocets, dwell in an artificial lagoon. Among the mammals are otters and aquatic rodents called "nutrias."

The reserve is close to the villages of Leiston and Saxmundham.

England:
Cornwall (36)

The southwestern coast of England juts out into the Atlantic Ocean forming the county of Cornwall. On the tip of this peninsula, over 309 miles (497 km) of trails provide nature lovers with a great opportunity to visit rocky or sandy shores and to see plants, birds, estuaries, dunes, and moors.

Along the coast there are the herring gull, the common gull, the kittiwake, the green cormorant, the guillemot, and the razorbill. The most colorful plants are the spring squill, the sea anemone, the wild carrot, and the Hottentot fig.

Wales:
Pembrokeshire (37)

This national park covers 161 sq. miles (418 sq. km). It includes 168 miles (270 km) of particularly rich and varied coast in southwestern Wales. It is possible to hike all the way through this stretch on a trail that offers breathtaking views of islands, estuaries, jagged coasts, brackish swamps, moors, and woods. Off the coast, the famous "bird islands," Skomer, Skokholm and Grassholm, host numerous nesting seabirds. On Grassholm, is found one of the largest colonies of gannets in the world. On Skokholm, about 20,000 pairs of Mediterranean shearwaters nest. Among the many other species along the coast are puffins, guillemots, razorbills, and Cornish choughs. Also to be seen are various ducks, geese, and shorebirds in the estuaries.

GLOSSARY

algae primitive organisms which resemble plants but do not have true roots, stems, or leaves. Algae are usually found in water or damp places.

amphipod small crustaceans such as beach fleas which feed off of epiphytic algae such as red or green seaweeds.

anadromous migrating up rivers from the sea to breed in fresh water.

arthropod any of numerous invertebrate organisms which has a hard, segmented outer shell and jointed limbs. Crabs, spiders, and scorpions are examples of arthropods.

baleen a type of whale which gathers food by means of a peculiar outgrowth of the upper jaws called a "baleen." Baleen is a horny material similar to fingernails, and forms plates in the mouth of the whale which are then used to filter plankton from the sea water.

bivalves animals that have shells consisting of two hinged parts. Oysters and clams are examples of bivalve mollusks.

byssus a mass of filaments or threads which certain bivalve mollusks use to attach themselves to fixed surfaces.

catadromous migrating down river to breed in marine water.

cetaceans fishlike aquatic mammals which breathe air from the atmosphere and are capable of regulating their body temperatures. Whales, dolphins, and porpoises are cetaceans.

chlorophyll a green pigment found in certain organisms that is used in the process of photosynthesis. This pigment is used to convert sunlight into energy.

cirri the feathery, modified legs of the barnacle. Cirri are well suited for filtering water and grasping microscopic food, which is then pulled inside the shell.

copepods tiny marine crustaceans. Copepods are members of the zooplankton community and are especially important because of their ability to avoid predators by migrating to safe waters when necessary.

deciduous forests forests having trees that shed their leaves at a specific season or stage of growth. Deciduous forests have long been exploited by man for the production of wood.

diatoms a group of single-celled plants which help to form phytoplankton. Diatom shells have spikes and ridges, and are often attached in long chains. This helps them to stay afloat in the water where sunlight can reach them.

dinoflagellates a group of single-celled plants (along with diatoms) that helps to form phytoplankton. Dinoflagellates can move about in the water with the help of two whiplike appendages called "flagella."

epiphyte a plant, such as red or green seaweeds, that grows on another plant upon which it depends for physical support but not for nutrients.

estuary the part of the wide lower course of a river where its current is met by the tides of the sea. Estuaries are places of silt expanses and brackish swamps, and provide homes for many complex and unique animal communities.

fleygastong a huge, triangular "butterfly net" fixed at the end of a long pole. Fleygastongs are used in the Faeroe Islands to trap puffins.

flocculation the process by which fine, floating silt particles attract each other and cling together in order to increase in size and weight and thereby sink to the sea floor.

gastropod a mollusk such as the periwinkle or limpet which is characterized by a single, usually coiled shell, and an abdominal muscle which serves as a means of movement.

habitat the area or type of environment in which a person or other organism normally lives or occurs. Specific environmental factors are necessary for providing a "natural" habitat for all living things.

humid containing a large amount of water or water vapor; damp. Warm air currents flowing through coastal areas produce a humid climate.

kelp any of various, often brown, seaweeds that grow on rocks immediately below the shore waters of the Atlantic coast. These seaweeds do not have roots, but grow by clinging tightly to the rocks.

leptocephalus one of the slender, transparent larvae of eels and certain other fish.

lichen primitive plant formed by the association of blue-green algae with fungi.

limpet the sea snail best able to withstand the violence of the waves along the Atlantic coast.

magma the molten matter under the earth's crust which is eventually released in a volcanic eruption. Magma originates from the shifting of tectonic plates deep within the inner layers of the earth.

nitrogen a colorless, tasteless, odorless gaseous chemical element forming nearly four-fifths of the atmosphere. Nitrogen is a component (part) of all living things.

nocturnal referring to animals that are active at night.

parr a young salmon during, which is under two years of age and living in fresh water. Parr learn to recognize the smell of the streams where they were born, so as adults they will know where to return when spawning time arrives.

peat partly decayed, moisture-absorbing plant matter found in ancient bogs and marshes, used as a plant covering or fuel.

photosynthesis the process by which chlorophyll-containing cells in green plants convert sunlight into chemical energy and change inorganic into organic compounds.

phycoerythrin a red pigment found in certain organisms that is used in the process of photosynthesis. This pigment is used to convert sunlight into energy.

phytoplankton small, floating aquatic plants. Phytoplankton is formed by huge quantities of microscopic algae adrift in the water and thrives only if sunlight filters through the water, allowing for photosynthesis.

pinnipeds carnivorous aquatic mammals which move about through the use of finlike flippers. Seals and walruses are examples of pinnipeds.

plankton plant and animal organisms, generally microscopic, that float or drift in great numbers in fresh or salt water.

salinity of or relating to the saltiness of something. The salinity of ocean water, for instance, varies in different regions and depths.

spermaceti a white, waxy substance consisting of various types of fatty acids. Spermacetti is obtained from the head of the sperm whale and used for making candles, ointments, and cosmetics.

tectonic plate one of several portions of the earth's crust which has resulted from geological shifting. The earth's plates have been moving continually for millions of years, causing new surface features and geological shapes.

tentacle an elongated, flexible, unsegmented protrusion or arm, such as those surrounding the oral cavity or mouth of the squid.

zooplankton floating, often microscopic sea animals.

INDEX